THE **LIVEABOARI**

THE
LIVEABOARD
GUIDE

TONY JONES

ADLARD COLES NAUTICAL • LONDON

Acknowledgements

Thank you to Ceri, without whom I would have sunk many times.
Photography by Tony Jones, Chris Beesley, Steve Rayner, Keith Pollitt,
Chris Sailsbury, Mark Wilson, Jo Bowling and Cabal. Thank you to all of the
photographers, boat owners, boating experts, liveaboards and everyone else
who provided insight, information and comments for this book.

Published by Adlard Coles Nautical
an imprint of Bloomsbury Publishing Plc
50 Bedford Square, London WC1B 3DP
www.adlardcoles.com

Copyright © Tony Jones 2012
First edition published 2012

ISBN 978-1-4081-4555-5
epub ISBN 978-1-4081-5925-5
ePDF ISBN 978-1-4081-5582-0

A CIP catalogue record for this book is available from the British
Library.

This book is produced using paper that is made from wood grown
in managed, sustainable forests. It is natural, renewable and
recyclable. The logging and manufacturing processes conform to
the environmental regulations of the country of origin.

Page layouts by Susan McIntyre
Typeset in 10.5 on 12.5pt URWGrotesk Light

Printed and bound in Spain by GraphyCems.

Note: while all reasonable care has been taken in the publication
of this book, the publisher takes no responsibility for the use of
the methods or products described in the book.

CONTENTS

INTRODUCTION

Welcome aboard! If you've just bought this book then I welcome you as a dear friend. If you're new to boat life this enthusiastic welcome may seem overgenerous, but if you spend enough time around boat folk you will come to cherish these friendly welcomes from people you might previously have considered strangers. That's just the way we are.

Making the decision to live aboard is the beginning of a very steep and never-ending learning curve. Don't let that worry you too much, though: boating and stress don't sit together well at all. You will find that there's plenty of help available for new boaters, and reading this book is a great place to start. You will quickly realise that there are many different ways to achieve a pleasurable liveaboard life, and the choices you make now will greatly influence your liveaboard lifestyle. The aim of this book is to help you create a liveaboard lifestyle that will suit you.

The first questions to ask yourself are 'Why do I want to live on a boat?' and 'Will boat life suit me? Most people who choose to live aboard will cite increased freedom, reduced living costs and a less complicated lifestyle among their reasons for choosing a boat for a home. Boat life can certainly deliver these rewards, but they come at a price. Living aboard can be very hard work, complicated and frustrating and has the potential to seriously affect your bank balance with expensive repairs and by restricting your earning potential. It's not all rolling countryside and the easy life. It is important to conduct some research beforehand and to be prepared for the ups and downs of life aboard a boat. It is all too easy to end up being bound to a complicated and expensive boating headache if you are not adequately prepared. The decision to live aboard is not one that should be made lightly or quickly and there is much to learn and consider if you intend to avoid the many potential pitfalls. But for those who have the right outlook on life and are willing to do their homework, a rewarding and peaceful lifestyle awaits.

This book focuses on the practical aspects of living aboard a boat and presents the pros and cons in all their glory. Alongside each chapter you will find stories, opinions, anecdotes and advice from a range of liveaboard boaters. Many of the boaters quoted here have lived aboard for a number of years. Their methods are tried and tested and their advice is grounded by experience and expertise. This may or may not work for you, but it will help you to determine whether you are suited to boat life and, more importantly, what kind of boat life is right for you.

Justine and Woody: *Frog With A Heart*   John: *Sound of Silence*

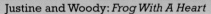

Boat folk

In every community there is a broad spectrum of characters and circumstances and boat life is no different. However, boating does seem to attract people of a specific type and there are some commonly encountered profiles. For example, it is common for boaters to live alone, mainly because of the space constraints of life aboard, but there is also a rambling 'free spirit' inherent in the lifestyle. Another reason for the prevalence of single boaters is that living aboard is sometimes a consequence of a divorce, leaving one partner (statistically usually the husband) with a share of equity large enough to buy a boat. That said, it is common enough for couples to live aboard too, especially as boat folk are often easy-going types who can rub along in the confines of a boat quite happily. Although not particularly common, you may find whole families living aboard. Usually these are small families comprising only three or four people, sometimes one parent, sometimes two, and usually only one or two kids.

   Young people may also become liveaboard boaters as they look for cheap places to live, while at the other end of the scale boat life is often the refuge of

Becky: *Summer Wine*

Jo and Troy from Snaygill Boats

the retired looking to downsize their life, sell their home and see out their days on the equity. Many of these retirees become constant cruisers, making good use of their new-found free time. However, growing old and infirm aboard a boat can be difficult and eventually very dangerous and it is important to have a contingency plan in place for when boat life is no longer a viable option.

Boat folk are a varied and eclectic bunch with many differing circumstances and lifestyles, but by reading this book you will see that there are a few common threads that unite us all.

Steve and Eileen: *Rahab*

Tony's Towpath Tales

One of the things that makes boat life so special is the sharing and considerate small-village-community culture that has almost disappeared from land-based living. Indeed, the canals are often referred to as one long, linear village community, and having spent time meeting people across the length and breadth of the system, it is easy to see why this is a fitting appraisal.

The boating community has come to my aid or pulled together to deal with a problem on many occasions, but one example sticks in my mind as being particularly exemplary. It occurred just a few days after I bought my boat as I was travelling south on the Grand Union Canal.

I had filled up my water tank before I left the marina, but somehow my cold-water tap in the galley was dry. Confused, I pulled alongside a water tap where a seemingly knowledgeable-looking chap was tinkering on his boat and asked for some advice. 'I'll bet you have two water tanks!' said the fellow, whose name turned out to be Danny. He went on to explain that sometimes boaters didn't like the look of the rust and cobwebs inside their old steel water tank and so installed a more hygienic plastic one beneath their front deck. After inserting the hose and turning on the tap, Danny and I settled into the easy conversation that can commonly be found with folk on the waterways. Almost half an hour and two cups of tea later I stepped into my boat and heard an alarming *splosh*! Instinctively I swore loudly, bringing Danny rushing over. Popping his head through the door he saw what was causing my alarm, and then he said the most beautiful words a man has ever said to me: 'Don't worry son, your boat isn't sinking.'

After a little investigation we found that the plastic tank was no longer watertight and so the water had been simply filling up the hull of my boat. Danny then spent a whole weekend helping me bail out the water, remove the ruptured tank and repair my plumbing. By way of thanks I offered to take Danny and his girlfriend out for dinner, but Danny would hear none of it. Even our two evenings spent at the pub were not a chance to reciprocate as Danny pointed out that this was his town and, while I was there, he would be buying the beers. 'You can buy the beers when I visit you,' said Danny. 'And I drink a lot!' he warned.

As the beer flowed I spoke to Danny about what it was like to live aboard, hoping to make the best of his expertise and experience. 'Let me tell you something about boat life,' he said. 'There is an old boating tradition that says you should never eat the last slice of bread. You should always throw it off the back of your boat for the ducks to eat. That way, when you are broke and you have no food and are on your arse with nothing to eat, there will always be a big fat duck hanging around near the back of your boat. All I'm doing here by helping you is throwing bread off the back of my boat. If you are going to make a success of living aboard I suggest that you do the same.'

His advice hit home and it has held me in good stead ever since.

Ask the Narrowboaters

Q – How did you come to live aboard a boat?

Sandra and Bob – *All Things Spanish*

My (Sandra's) great-great-grandfather was a boatman, taking boats on the Rochdale Canal between Manchester and Sowerby Bridge. I remember being told stories by my mother about his life and work, the stories being passed down to her from my grandmother. It was me that came up with the idea when we were planning our retirement. Bob was very enthusiastic about the prospect and began looking into it. Being a practical handyman type he loves fixing and making things – a useful skill when you live aboard. It suits us well.

Steve and Eileen – *Rahab*

We bought the boat as a retreat, a refuge from the hustle and bustle of modern life. Although we're not near retirement age just yet, our intention was to eventually get a bigger boat to live on when we retired. Before long we found ourselves spending more and more time on board until eventually we thought, 'Why wait?' So that was that! At first we were worried that if we lived aboard full-time the magic might wear off, but in fact quite the opposite has happened. Living aboard has its own joys and adventures that aren't apparent when you only use the boat occasionally.

Justine and Woody – *Frog With A Heart*

We had family and friends with boats and some of them lived aboard, so it was always on our radar as a housing option. With so much boating and liveaboard experience and advice we had a good idea of the features and fittings we thought we would like in a boat of our own. We spent a year travelling abroad and while we were away we designed our boat down to the last inch, ready to buy a sailaway shell when we got back.

HOW TO BUY A BOAT

Buying a boat is a very exciting business. Once the decision to live aboard has been made the compulsion to buy a boat immediately is overwhelming. At first glance there appear to be countless boats at bargain prices just waiting for you to float off into the sunset in, but of course there is much work and research to be done before you can be sure you have the right boat for the job. Good buying decisions are rarely made in haste, and the more time you spend doing research, the more likely you are to end up with the boat you want and need.

Types of boat

Although there are many different styles of boat to be found on the inland waterways there are some that are seen more frequently, and for good reason. While all of them could be used as a liveaboard vessel it is easy to see how some are more suited to that purpose than others. Bigger isn't always better!

Narrowboats

Narrowboats are the most popular choice for liveaboard boaters for reasons that will become obvious as you continue to read through this book. There are four main styles of narrowboat:

Traditional Stern – Just room for the tillerman

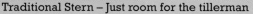

Cruiser Stern – Enough room to socialise

Traditional stern

Traditional stern narrowboats (or 'trads' as they are commonly called) have only a small aft deck just big enough for one person at the tiller. The engine room in this type of boat will be either just in front of the back deck or in a dedicated engine room in the middle of the boat, but in both cases it is inside the cabin.

Pros
✔ Considered by purists to look more authentic than other styles of boat
✔ Lots of internal, secure and lockable space
✔ Engine hole is covered and protected from rainwater

Cons
✘ Access into the cabin through the engine room can be tricky in some trad boats
✘ Access into the engine bay for repairs is also tricky in trad boats
✘ Little space for crew to socialise with the helmsman while under way
✘ Some kind of signalling system is required to communicate with crew inside the boat – for example, when approaching locks or bridges, or when in need of tea!

Cruiser stern

Cruiser stern boats feature a large back deck big enough for crew and passengers to socialise near the tiller when under way. The engine in a cruiser-style narrowboat will invariably be under this large back deck.

Tug Style – With a long bow deck

Semi Trad – The best (or worst) of both worlds

Pros
✔ Usually easy access into the cabin from the tiller
✔ Plenty of space for company to stand or sit with the helmsman near the tiller
Cons
✘ Rainwater will usually find a way into the engine hole and require occasional pumping out
✘ Reduced secure interior space

Semi-trad

Semi-trads enjoy the best (or worst) of both worlds, featuring the open space of a cruiser stern with the style benefits of the trad. The basic structure is the same as a cruiser-style boat, however the back deck is enclosed at the sides but has an open top.

Pros
✔ Looks like a trad at first glance
✔ Can accommodate company for the helmsman
Cons
✘ All the same negatives as a cruiser, but unlike a cruiser the deck is not practical for deckchairs

Tug

Tug-style boats have large, flat foredecks and are reminiscent of old working cargo boats. Sometimes these are covered with traditional canvas covers secured with ropes.

Pros
✔ They look fantastic
Cons
✗ The tug deck is useless for liveaboard purposes

Tony's Towpath Tales

My wallet was throbbing as I flicked through the pages of boats for sale on the Internet. As far as I could tell there were dozens of boats of around the right size and many were well within my budget. In fact, I could probably buy a boat and still have a fair amount of cash left over. Thankfully I had a friend with some considerable experience on hand to offer advice and to deter me from making bad decisions. Mike had been boating since 1977 and had lived aboard for several years. He was also aware that my compulsion to spend in haste might well cause me to repent, and would certainly compromise my leisure.

Firstly, I was advised against any boat that was less than 50ft long. While living on a smaller boat is possible, a large one is always more comfortable and convenient. Secondly, I was advised against buying any boat bigger than 59ft. Large boats have large running costs, and while the difference between a 59 footer and a 60 footer is negligible, Mike knew that once you break the 60ft threshold it is difficult to hold back. A long discussion was had about trads versus cruisers before we decided that internal lockable space was more useful than somewhere to sip Martinis with guests. Having filtered the field to include just those that qualified, there still appeared to be many boats well within my £30,000 budget. To cut a long story short, there was much debate before I was persuaded to spend £25,000 on the boat that Mike recommended instead of the £18,000 boat I coveted. 'Trust me,' Mike said. 'You'll thank me one day!'

And certainly I do. Back then I was not at all discerning about boat styling or fit-out quality and could not see £7,000 of difference between the two boats. Nowadays I look at my boat, the lines of its hull and the interesting character of the fit-out and I can see why Mike was so insistent. But I have to admit, I wasn't entirely convinced until he said, 'If you don't buy that boat, then I will!'

Wide beam

Leeds & Liverpool short boat

Vikings?

Narrowboats are occasionally called 'barges' by some, but canal folk in the know are quick to correct this mistake as a barge is a wider vessel with a beam over 6ft 10in. Others erroneously call them 'longboats' but thankfully Vikings are a rare sight on the cut.

Other boats

Although narrowboats are by far the most popular choice, plenty of other types of boats are suited to living aboard, some more so than others.

'Wide beam'

The style of wide beams is based upon that of the narrowboat and they are usually built by the same boatbuilders with the same features and equipment. Instead of having the standard width of 6ft 10in the wide beam boat will be over 10ft wide and sometimes as wide as 15ft. Wide beams are a relatively new concept and so predictably have modern-style interior fit-outs, but there are a handful of historically interesting wide beams still in existence, such as the Leeds & Liverpool Short Boats. With all the space of a small apartment, wide beams are popular with those whose primary focus is a comfortable home rather than extensive cruising as these boats cannot navigate the narrow canals on the network.

Dutch barge

Pros

✔ Lots more space with a more comfortable and conventional 'apartment' feel inside

Cons

✘ Limited cruising range due to their width

✘ Higher costs for mooring, licence and insurance

✘ Fewer boats with old-style character available

✘ Considered to be less classic and traditional by purists (unless you opt for a historically interesting vessel)

Dutch barge

These are a stylish alternative for those who want more space but still aspire to a classic style of boat. The most original Dutch barges are refurbished industrial or fishing vessels from Holland, but home-grown newly built Dutch barge-style boats are now available too.

Pros

✔ Beautiful classic-style boats with lots of character

✔ Wider with more interior space

✔ Ideal for cruising European rivers

Cons

✘ Limited cruising range caused by width, draft and wheelhouse height

✘ Increased mooring, licence and insurance costs

✘ Relatively more expensive than suitable liveaboard narrowboats

GRP cruiser

An unusual liveaboard boat

GRP cruisers and yachts

Although GRP (glass reinforced plastic) boats are seen frequently on the inland waterways they are mainly used for summertime leisure cruising and are rarely a choice for liveaboard boaters. The boats seen on canals are not usually large enough to accommodate a liveaboard lifestyle, nor are they easy to keep warm. That said, a handful of desperately hard-core GRP owners do live aboard their craft on canals, but most GRP liveaboards live at sea or, more rarely, on rivers.

The unconventional

You do occasionally see unusual and interesting boats used as liveaboards on the inland waterways. Small military, industrial and fishing vessels have enough space to be converted and often have interesting features and fit-outs. Such boats are usually owned by people with the necessary skills to maintain them, as unlike more traditional boats neither spare parts or support are readily available.

Go everywhere

To have access to the whole of the inland waterways network your boat should be no longer than 60ft and no wider than 6ft 10in. Beware of leaking lock gates though!

VAT

New boats are currently exempt from VAT if they are intended as your main home, although this is receiving some focus from HMRC and could very well change.

New or pre-loved?

The choice between new and used boats is not simply dictated by budget. While new boats do usually have a higher price tag, there are many other factors to consider too. Most new boats, like most new houses, are built to a template with little variation from an established theme. The shape of the hull, internal fit-out and the choice of facilities, utilities and equipment are usually set to the boatbuilder's stock style. As with new houses, most new boats are built to a tried-and-tested design, but the most prestigious builders do produce outstanding and beautiful boats – at a price.

Purchasing a new boat will usually mean waiting your turn in the builder's schedule. This could be anything up to a couple of years, particularly for boats by popular build companies, but if you aspire to your dream boat from a specific builder it is worth the wait. Another option is a 'sailaway', a new-build boat for sale at a stage of pre-completion. These can be anything from an empty steel shell to almost any stage of pre-completion. If you have the skills to fit out a boat yourself then these can be a great way to get your ideal boat at a bargain price. Be aware that fitting out a boat requires more than an average level of DIY competency; working on a boat is very different from working on a house in terms of method, skill set and regulations.

Financially speaking, buying a new boat can be rather complicated. Most experts recommend the enormously practical British Marine Federation staged-payment contract to efficiently manage the transaction and exchange of money. In addition, it is essential that both you and the builder have a complete understanding of exactly what features and additions you have ordered and how much they will cost. Visiting the builder at intervals to check progress is vital to ensure all is going to plan as mistakes and omissions can be difficult to correct retrospectively, and some mistakes are impossible to spot once the next stage of the build has begun. Bear in mind that it is not unusual for builders to miss the scheduled completion date, and at least one or two go bust each year, often leaving prospective owners out of pocket and with a heap of headaches.

Second-hand boats, like second-hand houses, have an inherent character installed by the string of previous owners. This character can make the boat either desirable or unattractive depending on both yours and the previous owner's tastes and requirements, but all older boats have a character that new boats off the conveyor belt will usually lack.

Used boats vary enormously. It is surprising how much variation can be installed into such a small space and how critical those variations can be for an aspiring liveaboard boater. The only way to appreciate the variety is to view and compare lots of boats, and the best way to do this is to visit one of the large brokerages. There are several large brokerages located around the country where it is possible to step aboard and view lots of boats in a single day.

Second-hand boats with a liveaboard heritage will often have useful features already built in and included in the price, such as powerful inverters, lots of storage space and fewer caravan-style convertible bunks. It is worth viewing boats both above and below your budget to get a good idea of what you can get for your money, but be prepared to be amazed at how prices can vary as if there is seemingly no science to the pricing process at all.

Str-e-e-e-tch

It is possible to 'stretch' a boat that is too short by adding a section into the middle. There is very little finesse to the process, which is done by simply sawing the boat in half before welding a new section of steel in the centre. The interior is then fitted out to make good inside. Very few boatyards take on this kind of work and very few owners consider it a good investment, preferring instead to buy a more suitable boat.

Ex-hire boats

Ex-hire boats are often available on the second-hand boat market. These boats will invariably have been kept looking tidy and most (but not all) will have enjoyed a strict and regular maintenance schedule. However, *all* ex-hire boats will have suffered a very hard life at the hands of inexperienced and often careless boaters. They will also be fitted out to be suitable for boat hire rather than for long-term liveaboard owners.

Ask the Narrowboaters

Q – What advice would you give to someone looking to buy their first boat?

John – *Sound of Silence*

If you are intending to renovate an old boat you had better make sure that you have a plentiful supply of three things: time, money and skill. Unless you are dedicated and proficient in many areas of DIY you should be wary of cheap boats that need lots of 'doing up'. These boats are a bargain for a reason and lots of people take on such projects only to sell them at a loss, still unfinished. If you are going to live aboard you would be advised to buy a boat you can step onto and start living on immediately, one that has all of the facilities you need. You can upgrade and make good in stages, but it is no fun living on a building site. Boat renovations always cost more than you budgeted for and always take longer than you expected.

How to find your ideal boat

There are several routes to explore when looking to buy a liveaboard boat and it would be wise to check them all before parting with your cash. Most boats that are for sale will have a sign in the window stating as much, and so a walk along the canal to see boats will often be the first step to whet your appetite. While there, you should speak with boaters and other waterways regulars too as the towpath telegraph is often the quickest and most reliable source of boating information and news. Boatowners, marina staff, boat hire companies and chandlers will usually have their finger on the pulse of what is happening locally.

Online

The largest selection of boats for sale can, of course, be found online. There are several large Web-based brokerages, and boats are often offered for sale on eBay. Checking online has many advantages: not only can it be done from the comfort of your armchair at no expense, but it is also a great way to swot up on the features and equipment you are likely to find when you view a boat in person. It is also a good way to get to grips with the technical jargon that is commonly used during the boat-buying process. Online listings sometimes include a diagram showing how the boat is laid out, details of facilities and features and a selection of photographs.

'Real life' boat brokerages

There are so many boats listed for sale on the Web that it is likely that you will buy your boat via one of these online brokerages. However, there is

Jo – Snaygill Boats

Hire a boat like the one you want and spend a couple of weeks living aboard. While this isn't quite the same as a long-term liveaboard life, it will give you a good idea of what it is like to live with the facilities you have. Can you get along with a cassette toilet or would you prefer a pump-out? Do you need a boiler or is a calorifier suitable? Knowing the answers in theory isn't the same as having experienced them up close and personal.

Justine and Woody – Frog With A Heart

If you have the skills and the time it is worth buying a sailaway. By doing the fit-out work ourselves we saved lots of money and came out at the end with a brand-new boat exactly to our perfect specifications. No compromises and all within a modest budget. The price you pay is the hard work that is necessary to do a good DIY fit-out.

Mike – Aldebaran

Unless you already have lots of boating experience, your dream boat will probably be the second boat you own, having noted the faults and imperfections of your first.

no substitute for stepping aboard and viewing boats in person. The vessels you look at online are likely to be found at locations scattered around the country, which makes viewing them logistically difficult, so a visit to a large 'real life' brokerage is always a good idea.

There are several sites around the country where you can view a large selection of boats all in one place. It is an enjoyable way to spend the day and there is always the possibility that you will find your ideal boat there, but be sure to compare many boats across a range of prices and styles before falling in love with one and making the decision to buy.

Boating press

Boats are also offered for sale in the popular boating magazines and newspapers. While there is less room for photographs and lengthy descriptions, these listings are still a good place to look to add to your list of 'possibles'.

Legwork

Only once you have seen a good range of boats will you be in a better position to discern a viable liveaboard from a selection of unsuitable ones. This is when the serious work begins as you can now arrange to view boats that could potentially become your liveaboard home. Murphy's Law states that boats which closely fit your ideal specifications will be moored many miles away, so it is worth being ruthless when deciding which to view. However, many boatowners have found their ideal boat in the most unlikely of places, and most fell in love after being flexible with their list of unconditional 'must have' features.

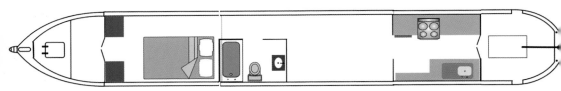

Aerial plan of *I Don't Believe It*

Paying for your boat

Suitable liveaboard boats start at around £15,000 for a serious 'doer-upper' and most cost significantly more. Many liveaboard owners purchased their boats using equity from the sale of a house, particularly those who sold and moved aboard in the early Noughties as property values were rising fast. Often those who sell their house to buy a boat are 'downsizing' either for economic or lifestyle considerations. It is fair to say that those who are actively seeking to enjoy a boating lifestyle are usually better suited to boat life than those who are forced aboard for purely financial reasons.

For boats at the cheaper end of the market, a personal loan is an option, but be aware that these boats might require some investment before they will be a comfortable and low-stress home. Marine mortgages are available for those who want to spend a little more than can be raised from a personal loan, and many boat brokerages can arrange these for you if you buy a boat from them. Be aware that marine mortgages can have comparatively high interest rates and are a secured loan, meaning that as with a house mortgage you can lose your

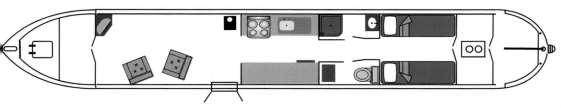

Aerial plan of *Barnaby*

home if you default on payments. Some even require home equity as an assurance and all will require a substantial deposit. It is also worth remembering that some liveaboard lifestyles can affect your bank balance, particularly if you move around a lot or have an expensive mooring near your place of work. All loans will need to be repaid and so it is important to factor in these specific boating issues.

Boat-buying checklist

- **Is the boat big enough?** Most liveaboard boaters agree that 45 to 50ft is a minimum comfortable-sized narrowboat for one person. Remember that bigger boats have bigger running costs for expenses such as moorings, licensing and maintenance.

- **Admin** When do the licence, boat safety and insurance certificates expire? If the expiry date on any of these is imminent it may be possible to negotiate on the price of the boat.

Underway

Many boatyards and marinas have boats for sale

- **Proof of ownership** Can the seller prove that the boat is theirs to sell? Ask to see their original receipt and some administrative history such as insurance and licence documents. Be sure to get a receipt/bill of sale when you hand over the money to buy the boat.

- **Survey** Do the sellers have a recent survey for you to look at? While it is likely that you will still need to commission a survey of your own prior to purchase, you can use the information from an old survey to help you decide if you are still interested enough to keep the boat on your list of possibles. When making an offer 'subject to survey' the seller may be more likely to contribute to any repairs the survey has highlighted if your offer was close to the original asking price. If a boat survey shows a thin or pitted hull steel thickness, that does not necessarily mean you should write it off. It is possible to overplate a boat, and while this is an expensive process, it may be a viable option for a suitably priced boat if the rest of the vessel is an attractive proposition.

- **Engine and gearbox** Make sure you take the boat out for a short cruise to check the engine and gearbox for problems. If you are not mechanically minded, be sure to take someone with you who knows what they are looking and listening for. Gearbox problems are common with narrowboats as the drive plates deteriorate through constant forward and reverse gear changing.

Waiting for the right boat to come along

- **Blacking** When was the boat last blacked? If it is due another coat of blacking soon this could be another price negotiation point. Get local quotes for blacking, including dry dock or haul-out costs, and negotiate accordingly.

- **Paintwork** A new external paint job is expensive. While few second-hand boats have pristine paintwork, be sure to take its condition into account when negotiating the price and working out a maintenance budget.

- **Resale value** Some boats depreciate in value more quickly than others, but it is difficult for new boaters to discern between a classically attractive boat and a mass-produced one. Outrageous paint jobs, quirky customisations and specialised adaptations will affect the value of a boat. Someone with lots of boating experience who does not have a vested interest in the sale is the best source of advice.

- **Refurbishment** If you are looking to move aboard immediately it is important that the boat you buy has everything you need in full working order. Heat, power, water and sanitation are essential from the moment you step aboard, so make sure these utilities do not need a major overhaul. While it is reasonable to expect to do a little refurbishment, if you can't step aboard and start living immediately, your liveaboard dream could become a delayed and expensive headache.

2

WHEREVER I LAY MY HAT

It is often said that finding a suitable mooring is one of the biggest challenges facing boatowners, and with living aboard becoming an increasingly popular lifestyle choice, suitable moorings are in high demand. A common piece of advice for new boaters is to secure a mooring even before you buy a boat, but this in itself can be problematic. Most marinas sell mooring space by the foot and so it makes economic sense to put the longest boat possible into the space that they have available. The first question you will be asked when enquiring about moorings is 'How big is your boat?', and without a conclusive answer you may be asked to enquire again when you have bought one. One way to get around the problem is to reserve and pay for a mooring space large enough for your prospective boat and be prepared to swallow the extra cost if the boat you eventually purchase is smaller. However, buying a boat can take time and, as stated before, should not be rushed, and so parting with cash month after month for a mooring spot you are not using flies in the face of frugal boating.

If you do buy the boat before finding a suitable mooring you will need to move quickly and will probably have to make greater compromises in order to do so. You might fall lucky and be able to secure a good mooring straight away, but there is always the risk that no convenient spots are available, leaving you mooring on the towpath until space becomes free, and this can take months or even years in popular locations. Lingering on visitor moorings and 'bridge hopping' (see

Ask the narrowboaters

Q – How did you get your mooring?

Steve and Eileen – *Rahab*
Our first mooring came with the boat when we bought it. While it was expensive and not particularly convenient for us, we did at least have a mooring, so we could look for something more suitable at our leisure. It wasn't until we found our current mooring spot that we decided that living aboard was viable. We found the boat club where we currently moor as we were walking up the towpath. There was a sign with a phone number, which we called, and three months later we were moored there and living aboard. One of the things we like about our new mooring is that our boat is not too far from the car park. At the last place it was quite a walk and carrying shopping between the two was a nightmare. To make matters worse, the path was paved with gravel, which meant that pulling a trolley was almost impossible. We didn't live aboard at that stage, so it wasn't too much of a problem, but I'd hate to have to go through that ordeal regularly as a liveaboard.

page 37 Free moorings) will soon attract the attention of British Waterways agents, and so the prospect of this being your only option should not be taken lightly.

The big issue

Official residential liveaboard moorings are costly and extremely rare. Marinas wishing to offer residential moorings need to apply for and be awarded proper planning permission, and in many areas this type of planning status for 'dwellings' is prohibited. Even when planning permission is granted, it is often applied specifically to a single boat or a specific mooring spot and is not transferable; even if a marina has planning permission for residential mooring in one spot, they usually need to reapply should there be a need to change either the boat or the specific mooring spot. Those boaters who do secure a residential spot potentially have all of the amenities of a land-based home, including a postcode and postal service, a telephone landline and sometimes the opportunity to pay council tax too! However, liability for council tax is ambiguous where liveaboard boaters are concerned, and the Residential Boat Owners Association has defended several cases where liveaboards have been faced with a bill. The general rule is that if the terms of your mooring stipulate that your boat is likely to be moved to a different mooring spot, you are not liable for council tax.

Most mooring providers, though, do not offer official residential moorings, and while some will strictly enforce a no-liveaboard policy, others will 'unknowingly' accommodate discreet liveaboards. Even some marinas owned by British Waterways offer a 'Class A' or 'Class 1' mooring which entitles boaters to stay on their boat all year. The definition of 'residential' is so

Pontoon style moorings

Pontoon power point

Face to face

It is rarely fruitful to enquire about moorings by phone or email. It may be necessary to set up an appointment by phone, but don't enquire about costs or space, and certainly do not declare your liveaboard status. Face-to-face meetings are always preferable, particularly when the mooring provider has a policy of vetting new arrivals.

ambiguous that it is easy for marina owners to find a loophole, especially when, as is usually the case, most boats leave the marina for some weeks or months during the course of any given year and so their owners cannot be accurately described as permanent residents.

It is wise to do some research and look for signs that people live aboard before meeting with the owner or manager of the site. Ask other boaters about the local liveaboard options, but avoid asking boaters from the site you are coveting until you know how the land lies. When a meeting has been arranged be careful about asking 'Can I live aboard here?' as the answer is often an official no, but there is usually a way to achieve an unspoken understanding. Some will ask outright if you live aboard and explain that living on site is not allowed and that you must vacate

Justine and Woody – *Frog With A Heart*

We had plenty of time to find a marina while our boat shell was being built, which is just as well as we had to find a mooring where we would be allowed to work on the boat. Some marinas have very strict rules and so it was important to get permission for us to be banging and sawing. The mooring was at a modern marina where boats are moored close together on long, thin floating pontoons. We paid for six months of mooring fees in advance and were determined to get out of there as soon as that time was up. Although it was a nice enough place, mooring somewhere like that with boats packed in tightly together was not the boating lifestyle that we aspired to. We set off onto the cut with the intention of cruising around until we found a better mooring. For one reason and another we ended up continuous cruising, and quite happily too.

your boat for a set number of days per year, while others have a higher tariff for 'high-use' boats. Answering questions honestly and complying with the rules laid down by the site is always the best policy to avoid issues further down the line. It may be that you can comply with the regulations by taking your boat out to cruise the local waterways for a few weeks or months each year. This is a most agreeable means of toeing the line, and as long as you do not hog popular visitor moorings you are unlikely to attract the attention of BW agents. (Boaters with a permanent mooring seem to attract less attention than those registered as continuous cruisers for some reason.) Perhaps your partner is based locally and you spend occasional nights there? A few weeks of holiday later and you will almost certainly have negated any enforceable definition that you live at your marina.

Moorings providers are not obliged to give you a mooring and so you should make your application as attractive as possible. Some places, clubs and private marinas especially will discriminate against untidy looking boats with the view that these will 'lower the tone' of the establishment. A boat roof lined with piles of firewood, pushbikes, loud unruly dogs, a TV ariel and bags of rubbish can hint that not only are you likely a liveaboard, but likely a messy one at that. Presenting a good image and reading between the lines when discussing moorings can make the difference between their site being full and them being able to squeeze your boat in somewhere.

When looking for a mooring there are so many factors to consider that it is inevitable that you will need to compromise somewhere, but by being flexible and objective a solution can usually be found. In an ideal world you would find a friendly, perfectly located and well-managed mooring with great security in a beautiful location with great facilities and lots of accessible local resources. And it would be inexpensive too. In reality you will probably need to compromise and your

Online moorings

Step aboard

When buying a boat, ask if the mooring can be transferred to you as the new owner. Some mooring providers are eager to do this as it means they will not be losing money while they look for another boat to fill the empty spot. This is often the easiest way to start, and even if the location is less than ideal it buys some breathing space while you look for a more convenient spot. Beware of contracts that tie you down for a long period of time, though.

Fat wallets

Most mooring providers will charge extra to moor a wide beam, sometimes double the price of a narrowboat.

Boatyard facilities

Boatyard moorings will often have invaluable dry dock or crane-out facilities on site. Wide beam owners should be aware that dry dock facilities for wide boats are less frequently available and crane costs can be more expensive too.

Quote

Jo – Snaygill Boats
We do not have planning permission to offer residential moorings and so cannot accommodate liveaboards, but every now and again it becomes evident that someone is living aboard on site. Of course, we understand that boaters will occasionally overnight here, but we are always clear when we welcome new boaters that we cannot accommodate liveaboards. It is awful when you realise that a new customer has been less than honest when claiming they do not live on their boat.

personal circumstances will dictate which of these areas you can be most flexible in. It will come as no surprise that you will usually get what you pay for.

Pay to stay

Large, commercially run purpose-built marinas are popping up everywhere. Most will offer the basic utilities a liveaboard boater will need, such as electricity hook-up, water point and usually a pump-out station. Some feature a separate shower and toilet block, and occasionally a marina will boast laundry facilities, parking, chandlery supplies and even wireless Internet access. These features, coupled with the location, will dictate the price you pay. Most marinas of this type have floating-pontoon access and boats are moored close together, but rarely abreast. There is usually an on-site manager and most managers will, ironically, live aboard on site.

A short distance from any large marina you will find a boatyard and these are usually a cheaper mooring option where space is available. Being a working boatyard the premises will invariably have a more 'industrial' ambiance, and it is worth remembering that working with steel boats is often a noisy business. Moorings at facilities like this are often supplementary to the main boatyard business and boats will be packed into every available space. Often they will be moored two and sometimes three or more abreast. Facilities are often limited. Electricity supply may come via a cable run from the nearest power point, and filling with water might mean shuffling boats to the nearest tap. Don't be surprised if you need to visit the nearby large marina to get a pump-out. That said, moorings at boatyards have the benefit of knowledgeable and handy boat maintenance experts on site, and while you should not expect a discounted rate for working on your boat, you will often receive preferential treatment.

Another less frequently available option is a boat club mooring and these can be surprisingly good value for money. Boat clubs are usually run as a not-for-profit organisation and manage to keep fees low because boaters are expected to contribute to the upkeep of the club, negating the need to pay management and staffing costs or turn a profit. Most clubs have a long and proud history and many have evolved from humble beginnings on the towpath to a point where many have the best facilities available, often including a clubhouse of some description. Boat clubs usually have a strong social ethos with all of the pros and cons inherent in any close-knit community. This means that club members tend to stay members for many years and moorings are not frequently available as a result. Most clubs run an extensive waiting list.

Waterside private landowners sometimes offer moorings as a small enterprise, usually for only a handful of boats. Predictably, the facilities provided vary widely from site to site and are unlikely to feature boating-specific services. Interestingly, one such site fell under the care of the local council who, upon realising the site was home to liveaboard boaters, set about legitimising the residential status of the moorings. By charging the lowest rate of council tax the moorings became bona fide residential, thus eliminating the earlier ambiguity and subterfuge.

On-line mooring, ie being moored on the canalside, is one of the cheapest mooring options as these moorings usually have no facilities at all. While this might sound like the worst possible option, on-line moorings have several distinct advantages. Firstly, they are usually cheap, and so if that is a primary focus for you then on-line mooring might be your best option. Secondly, as a bona fide mooring you will not have to worry about being moved on in the same way that

Security

On-line moorings are often situated on the towpath, where the general public have access. While security is not often an issue where moored boats are a familiar sight, it is worth checking whether there is a regular local problem. No mooring is totally secure and problems can potentially occur anywhere. A good boating community is usually enough to discourage all but the most hooligan of elements.

Pontoon mooring

continuous cruisers often will. Thirdly, this type of mooring is widely available and often in the most surprisingly picturesque of locations. And lastly, you will usually have boating neighbours on the same stretch of canal, amounting to a ready-made community.

Of course, without an electrical hook-up it is important that you have an engine and an electrical system that you can rely on, but this should be true of all boaters. Similarly, the need to travel for pump-out and water should not be too much of an inconvenience for boaters who are well organised and prepared, and most will relish the opportunity to start their engines and undertake some actual boating, no matter how short or irregular.

Short-term moorings

Many marinas and boat clubs will offer short-term moorings for set periods during the year. These are available because a regular moorer is away cruising for a given period and filling the space is a good way to earn extra revenue. Some places offer moorings during winter as people hunker down after the cruising season, and it is worth securing these as early as possible.

Typical liveaboard

Water point

On-line moorings are most frequently available directly through British Waterways and have recently required a tender by sealed auction bid. It is possible to get a bargain if you aspire to a mooring location that is less popular for some reason, and it is often advisable to check demand and prices with others at the site.

Many boaters aspire to own their own mooring, either at the end of a garden or by owning a piece of land next to the water. These types of mooring are rare and usually have limited facilities. British Waterways will charge a fee to moor on their water, usually 50% of the fee levied for similar moorings in that vicinity. If you do not own the land then you will probably need to add a profit for a landowner. It can quickly become an expensive and poorly provided option, but for boaters where privacy and solitude are important this can be boating Utopia – your own place, your own rules and (almost) no one to answer to.

Free moorings

Yes, it is possible to incur no mooring costs whatsoever, but there is a different price to pay. Visitors' moorings are available at thousands of places on the waterways network and there is no charge for staying there. It is also possible to moor at the water's edge where this is practicable and the land is not privately owned. However, these moorings are not permanent and the amount of time you are allowed to stay there ranges from a maximum of 14 days to as little as just a few hours. These visitors' moorings are intended as just that.

Boats without a permanent mooring are termed 'continuous cruisers' and there are rules governing the mooring activities of this type of boat. A continuous cruise

Quote

Troy – Snaygill Boats

'In the last few years the number of people enquiring about liveaboard moorings has increased sharply and we know that other marinas and boatyards are experiencing the same thing. Living aboard is gaining popularity fast!'

is a slightly ambiguous activity, but the craft used is defined by British Waterways as a 'boat [that] travels widely around the waterway network without staying in any one place for more than 14 days (or less where local BW signs indicate a shorter period)'. The specifics are not set in stone, and while BW have done their best to define the rules for continuous cruisers, there are many boaters who endeavour to inhabit a grey area within the regulations.

The rules state that the boat must move to a new location at least every 14 days, with a 'new location' being defined as a new district rather than a different mooring spot in the same area. The guidance states: 'The necessary movement from one neighbourhood to another can be done in one step or by short gradual steps. What the law requires is that if 14 days ago the boat was in neighbourhood X, by day 15 it must be in neighbourhood Y. Thereafter, the next movement must normally be to neighbourhood Z, and not back to neighbourhood X (with obvious exceptions such as reaching the end of a terminal waterway or reversing the direction of travel in the course of a genuine progressive journey).'

Continuous cruisers needing to be in a particular area (usually for work) will often resort to what is known as 'bridge hopping', moving short distances in a given area before returning to the original location at some future point. This

Factors to consider

- Location
- Electricity
- Water
- Pump-out
- Gas, coal and other supplies
- Local cruising options
- Train/bus services
- Shopping
- Chandlery
- Crane or dry dock
- Boat maintenance
- Laundry
- Shower or toilet block
- Internet access
- Clubhouse
- Post collection service

An undercover dry dock facility

is rarely a successful strategy and will soon attract close attention from BW enforcement staff, the resultant stress being a veritable coffin nail in the carefree boating lifestyle most of us aspire to. The only way to avoid the hassle is to abide by the rules and move to a new neighbourhood every 14 days. The definition of a 'neighbourhood' varies with geography and not by mileage. In urban areas a new neighbourhood might be the next town a short distance away, whereas in rural areas the distance could be far greater, and this is where some boaters feel there is a grey area. 'A sensible and pragmatic judgement' is required according to the BW's guidelines.

The mooring rules are overseen by enforcement staff from British Waterways, whose interpretation of the regulations seems to vary enormously according to reports from boaters from across the country. Specifically allocated visitors' moorings are more strictly enforced, as are the stopping places on all of the busy parts of the network. Patrols are less frequent on quieter and less desirable stretches of water, but consistently stubborn overstayers will soon attract attention.

More information about mooring regulations can be found on-line at http://www.britishwaterways.co.uk/license-it/boating-essentials/mooring-information.

Tony's Towpath Tales

My boat was lying in Daventry, Northamptonshire, when I bought it. I didn't move aboard immediately and stayed for a few weeks in the place I was renting in Surrey while I searched for a mooring nearer my work in Epsom. Having commissioned the marina in Daventry to do some work on my boat's electrical system I had a few weeks of grace to find a more convenient mooring. Eventually I found a space in a large commercial marina located on the beautiful River Wey near Woking. This solved my immediate mooring issue, but in turn raised several other problems to be faced at a later date. The most immediate of these was that the River Wey is managed by the National Trust and living aboard is simply not allowed. I was informed in no uncertain terms that living aboard would not be tolerated, and told stories of people who had tried to get away with it only to be confronted by the National Trust. Luckily, my circumstances at the time allowed me to get around the problem in a variety of ways. I still had use of my rented land home for a few more weeks and my girlfriend lived close enough to the marina to be convenient. Add to that three weeks of holiday spent abroad and a period where the boat was having yet more work done and I managed to make my stopovers on the boat sporadic enough to not attract any attention for the several months I was moored there.

The second problem was financial. The cost of mooring at the marina was eye-wateringly expensive, with the annual mooring fee for my boat being in excess of £4,000. For that price I could have a residential mooring elsewhere on the network, let alone a strictly enforced non-liveaboard spot. The price was certainly reflected in the quality of the mooring and the beauty of the venue, though, which brings me onto another problem I was now faced with. By the time I had spent a few nights aboard my boat in the beautiful setting that surrounded my mooring I knew I needed a more convenient liveaboard spot as soon as possible. The River Wey is one of the most stunning waterways in the UK, and after a very short time I was sold on boat life hook, line and sinker. I had a choice: I could stick around in Surrey and keep my job, but not be able to live on my boat, or I could quit my job and set off north to some place where mooring and living aboard would be easier. So I headed north with the intention of finding a mooring (and hopefully some work) somewhere en route.

A busy boatyard mooring

The idea of living in London has never really floated my boat and so I had no intention of finding a stopping there, but I still wanted to live in the south. Having reached the Grand Union Canal I stopped in Hemel Hempstead, Hertfordshire, to enquire about moorings. Immediately I was asked if I lived aboard, to which I replied that I worked away regularly and stayed with my girlfriend often, but would be staying on my boat for periods of time in between. This seemed to satisfy the mooring manager, and I was given a spot costing approximately half of what I was paying on the River Wey; and there I stayed for over a year, venturing out occasionally to cruise the waterways around the area. Again, my frequency aboard did not seem to concern anyone who might care that I was living there, and I was never troubled about it.

THE COST OF BOATING

'A boat is a hole in the water into which you throw money.'

Aspiring boaters often ask about the financial aspects of boating. Despite the stock response being 'an arm and a leg and your firstborn child!' it is a difficult question to answer given the enormous variety of boats and boaters and the various different types of waterways. To get some idea of the costs involved, a handful of boaters were asked to keep track of their boating-related spending for a whole year, listing everything from the mandatory licence fee right down to the last firelighter, windlass and emergency repair bill. The costs listed are true of 2011 and will of course vary over time. Here is a summary.

The big three

Licence

Most canals and rivers in the UK are managed by either British Waterways or the Environment Agency and can be navigated upon purchasing a Gold Licence. A handful of navigable waterways are managed by other organisations and so are not covered by the Gold Licence; a list of these can be found below. A Standard Licence covers all of the canals and rivers specifically managed by BW, covering a choice of either England and Wales or Scottish waterways. This licence is sufficient for the vast majority of boaters, and any occasional forays outside its range can be covered by short-term licences from the appropriate authority (see below for example costs). Boaters who are happy to restrict their cruises to just BW-owned rivers can buy a Rivers Only Licence and these cost less than the others mentioned above.

The length of your boat is used to calculate the cost of the licence (the beam width is not a factor here), with discounts applying for prompt payment and a surcharge of £150 if payment is received late.

For more information visit www.britishwaterways.co.uk/licence-it, but here are two examples.

- *The Watchman* is 50ft long and has a 12-month England and Wales Standard Licence. This would cost £669.60 but was discounted for prompt payment to £602.64.
- *Aldebaran* is 60ft long and has a 12-month Gold Licence costing £1,043 paid in full in advance.

Visitors licence fees (50ft narrowboat)

1 day on the Thames – £26 (Note: length and beam are considered.)

3 days on the Basingstoke Canal – £27.15

1 week on the River Wey – £56 (Lock tolls included.)

Cruise the length of the Manchester Ship Canal – £128 (Conditions apply. Call for details.)

Boat safety certificate

Boats are tested for safety by qualified inspectors every four years and compliant craft are issued a boat safety certificate. The test points are identical for all boats irrespective of size or type, and so these variables will not affect the cost to any great degree.

The safety examination is a very black and white affair and therefore quite easy to budget for. Although the cost of the test is not fixed, most inspectors will charge around £150, which will cover the examination and the issue of the certificate. Most fail points can be remedied with minimal financial cost and a couple of man-hours, although non-compliant gas cookers are sometimes more easily replaced than repaired. Some examiners may make an additional charge if a second visit is required following a fail, particularly if they have any distance to travel.

Other licensing agencies (non BW/EA)

The Basingstoke Canal	Basingstoke Canal Authority Tel: 01252 370073
River Wey	The National Trust Tel: 01483 561389
River Avon	Avon Navigation Trust Tel: 01386 552517
The Norfolk & Suffolk Broads	The Broads Authority Tel: 01603 610734
Bridgewater Canal (Manchester)	Bridgewater Canal Company Ltd Tel: 0161 629 8266 (for visits over 7 days)
Manchester Ship Canal	Harbour Master's Department Tel: 0151 327 1461

Insurance

Like all insurances the price is dependent on risk and the amount of cover required. Rod Daniel of Craftinsure shed a little light on the dark art of boat insurance: 'The value and age of the boat are key premium factors rather than the length or beam width. Other factors to consider include where the boat is based and any additional cover you might require for boat contents. If you live aboard you can expect to pay more. Although liveaboard boats are less likely to be left unattended for long periods, increased use and the value of items on board do tend to add to the risk.'

Avoiding tidal waterways and opting for a higher excess can reduce your insurance costs, but price is not the only consideration. The current financial climate may encourage boaters to cut costs, but it is important to ensure that your insurance provides adequate cover. Some insurers will ask for a survey if your boat is over 20 years old. This can add £400 to your insurance expenditure once crane/dry dock costs are included, although this survey will usually be valid for insurance for five years.

Moorings

Moorings costs are dependent on geography, facilities and the size of your boat. Moorings with facilities such as mains electricity, local pump-out/Elsan or laundry will cost more than a basic on-line mooring, as will moorings in picturesque or convenient locations. Most marinas will also charge different fees if moored alone or abreast another boat, and some also differentiate between frequent and infrequent usage.

Some insurance quotes examples

(courtesy of craftinsure.com)

Boat	60ft x 12ft wide beam	57ft semi-trad narrowboat	30ft cruiser stern narrowboat	25ft GRP river cruiser
Value	£130	£50,000	£15,000	10,000
Build	2008	1996	1971	1979
Approximate quote	£458 pa	£175 pa	£115 pa	£110 pa

(All quotes assume no previous claims, zero no-claims bonus and £150 excess.)

Case studies: Moorings

Airedale Boat Club near Bingley sits on the Leeds-Liverpool Canal, a stone's throw from the famous Five Rise Locks staircase. A 50ft narrowboat on a breasted narrow-beam mooring costs £14 per foot per annum (£700 per year). ABC has electricity supply and water is available from a BW tap on the towpath opposite. Pump-out and Elsan disposal are a short walk away. The club is run as a not-for-profit organisation and boatowners meet regularly to carry out maintenance chores around the site to keep mooring fees low. Membership costs £7.50 per year.

On-line moorings with limited facilities are a prolific and relatively cheap mooring option. An offside mooring to accommodate a 40ft boat at Cowley South near Uxbridge on the Grand Union went at tender for £1,271 per annum earlier this year. Apart from the provision of mooring rings and gated access, this mooring site has no additional facilities, although water and pump-out/Elsan are both within 15 minutes' cruising time.

Apsley Marina can be found on the Grand Union Canal near Hemel Hempstead. It is operated by BWML (a British Waterways company) and was opened in 2003. Facilities include metered electricity, water points, showers, pump-out and Elsan, and a laundry facility too. Nestling among a modern apartment block complex, a residential mooring here will cost £5,412 per annum.

Pyrford Marina is part of the Tingdene group. It is a fine example of a modern commercial marina with extensive facilities and an on-site engineer. The River Wey is owned and maintained by the National Trust and boats moored here enjoy a stunningly beautiful setting; however, the Trust does not allow residential moorings anywhere on the river. Facilities include metered electricity, water point, pump-out and Elsan, toilets and shower block, dry docking and diesel. At £66.94 per foot per annum a 72ft boat on a standard mooring would cost £4,819.68, with an option to pay by monthly direct debit at additional cost.

Engineer's Wharf can be found on the Paddington Arm of the Grand Union Canal in London on a 26 mile lock-free section of the London canal network and is a good example of a top-of-the-range premium mooring. Matthew Bannister, BW's West London moorings co-coordinator, said, 'Whilst location is an important factor, I believe the range of facilities at Engineer's Wharf is an equally attractive feature. The land required to build such extensive and attractive facilities is in short supply in the capital and so there is a high demand for moorings such as those at Engineer's Wharf.'

Facilities at Engineer's Wharf include:

- Secure serviced pontoon moorings
- Offline basin location offering 20 narrowboat berths
- Private berth holders' toilets and showers
- Five conveniently spaced pump-out facilities
- Up to 32 amp electrical supply
- Dedicated under-cover storage area
- Excellent access to London's waterways

A residential mooring here was recently won by tender at a price of £9,250 per annum. It is important to remember that residential moorings are subject to council tax charges.

Pyrford marina. Photo by Jo Bowling

Boat licence

Utilities

Utilities costs will vary with usage and a liveaboard boater will obviously spend more than a weekender or holiday cruiser.

Mains supply costs for electricity are cheaper than domestic house charges as most marinas will purchase electricity in bulk. Marinas cannot charge a premium to their customers as they are not regulated energy suppliers, so this discount is passed on to us down the line.

Water provision is included in the licence fee and so there is no extra expense here, although some boaters use filtration systems or water purification tablets at a small additional cost.

Gas bottles come in several sizes, with the larger ones offering better value, but most boat gas lockers seem to accommodate the 13kg canisters. In addition to the gas used for cooking, some boats have gas-powered instantaneous water heaters. These increase consumption considerably, though most boaters consider this a small price to pay for instant hot water.

Winter warmth

The vast majority of boats use a multi-fuel stove for heat. The debate rages continually over which coal is best, and boaters are usually partisan and eager to compare costs and performance. Many will endeavour to find a timber yard or similar source for free or cheap kindling. While fallen dead wood can be found on and around the towpath, one should consider the impact this has on local wildlife. Many types of insect use rotting dead wood as either food or habitat, and so plundering this natural resource for your fire is frowned upon by naturalists as intensive harvesting can quickly lay waste to an area.

Some boats make the most of the heat produced by their stove to provide hot

Boatyards and marinas offer many different services

Gas for cooking, heating and refrigeration

Case studies: Utilities costs

Tony – *The Watchman*
'I often work from my boat and so I have quite a high usage, particularly electricity to charge my laptop and phone.'
Gas: (gas boiler & cooker) – 12 x 13kg canisters @ £24
             = £288 per annum.
Electricity: 240v appliances: fridge, laptop, CD player, mobile phone
             charger = £180 per annum.

Becky – *Summer Wine*
'I rarely cook aboard, so my gas usage is quite low.'
Gas: Cooker = £21.40 per annum.
Electricity: 240v appliances: fridge, microwave, mobile phone
             charger, television, hairdryer, portable electric heater
             = £70 per annum via token-fed mains electricity meter.

Lindsay – *Cerian*
'We always make a point of switching off the boiler pilot light. You'd be surprised how much gas can be saved this way. I find the gas-powered fridge is more cost-effective than an electrical one too.'
Gas: Gas-powered refrigerator, water heater and central heating
             = £72 per annum.
Electricity: £30 per annum via token-fed mains electricity meter.

water and to heat radiators by utilising a back burner system. This is an efficient way to get 'free' hot water during wintertime, but lighting the stove is not practical during summer.

Diesel-fuelled heaters are another option. There are several types to choose from but most are fed from the same diesel tank as the boat's engine, making running costs difficult to obtain. Once installed, most diesel stoves have very low maintenance costs, but some types of diesel-fuelled heaters will require regular servicing. Jason Kaye of BK Marine Systems specialises in servicing Eberspacher and Webasto diesel-fuelled heaters and was keen to address their reliability issue. 'The units have a two-year warranty from new and I wouldn't expect them to need any attention at all in this time. After a few years of use I advise that people get a routine service done every couple of years at least, and possibly yearly in high-usage applications such as liveaboard boats. More frequent problems are likely due to poor installation or poor-quality fuels. A standard service kit plus labour will usually not break the £200 mark.'

Case studies: Coal and kindling usage

Debbie – *Dunster* – Debbie and her family live aboard their boat and have access to free seasoned dead wood through her work = £140 per annum.

Becky – *Summer Wine* – Becky stays aboard her narrowboat near her workplace during the week = £284.30 per annum.

Mike – *Aldebaran* – Mike and his family use their boat for weekends and extended cruises and enjoy cruising during the winter = £90 per annum.

Only for boaters

Fuel usage

Diesel fuel expenditure is difficult to estimate as usage and prices vary so widely. Although many keep a log of the fuel they purchase, few keep records of engine running hours. Recent legislation taxes fuel for boats differently depending on how it is used.

Fuel for propulsion is taxed at a higher rate than that used to charge batteries for domestic use or for diesel-powered heating. For those with a single fuel tank it is impossible to accurately measure the proportions of fuel used for each, and so a sensible approximation is usually implemented. 'After much discussion within

Diesel prices vary greatly

Save money with eco friendly solar power

Case studies: Fuel usage

Tony – *The Watchman* – 91 litres diesel (70 engine hours).

Lyndsay – *Cerian* – 141 litres diesel (132 engine hours).

Becky – *Summer Wine* – 219 litres diesel (220 engine hours).

the industry it has become almost standard practice to implement a 60/40 split when selling red diesel for boats,' says Troy of Snaygill Boats. 'Customers sign a declaration of usage which we keep on file for HMRC to view if requested.'

It is the responsibility of the boatowner to accurately declare their usage proportions for tax purposes, and it is entirely legal to purchase diesel at domestic tax rates if the boat will use the fuel while moored, during the winter, for example. It is also worth noting that HMRC does not require fuel suppliers to record fuel sold in volumes of less than 100 litres, although many keep records of all sales, regardless of volume sold.

Case studies: Pump-outs

Tony – *The Watchman* – 10 x pump-outs @ £12.50 = £125.00 per annum.

Becky – *Summer Wine* – 8 x pump-outs @ £10–£12.50 = £90 per annum.

Lyndsay – *Cerian* – 2 x pump-outs @ £15.00 = £30.00per annum. ('We have a huge black water tank!')

Pump-outs

The main factors governing pump-out costs are frequency (of boat use) and volume (of your black water tank). Many boaters negate this cost by utilising cassette-type toilets as these are free to empty at Elsan sanitary disposal points. Both pump-out and cassette owners will utilise odour-neutralising solutions but this cost is negligible, totalling approximately £20 per annum. Replacements, spares and repairs are listed in the maintenance section of this article and are thankfully rare.

Boat maintenance

How long is a piece of string? Maintaining one's boat is a major expenditure and the costs incurred here can vary enormously. Not only is the age and condition of your boat a factor but the prices charged by companies providing services can differ hugely too.

Some maintenance issues creep up slowly, while breakdowns can come from nowhere and require immediate attention. While it is difficult to know what's around the corner, there are some constants to bear in mind when budgeting for boat maintenance, such as replacement batteries, water pumps and stern gland packing. These are consumable items with high workloads and will invariably go wrong at the most inconvenient moment, and so budgeting for them makes a lot of sense. Leisure batteries can cost anything from £70 and a new water pump will set you back around £100. Overhauling a stern gland will cost less than a tenner but is a greasy, time-consuming job.

Engine servicing is usually carried out yearly with a view to avoiding breakdown expenses later. A basic service – changing oil, filters, coolant and spark plugs – will cost around £150, and a more thorough going-over to take account of glow plugs and valves can set you back over £250. It may be worth learning to service your engine yourself, not only to save on labour costs but also to nurture your relationship with your boat: the cost of replacing the consumable filters and fluids comes in at around £80. If you have an older engine you may want to keep a small pot of extra cash to make available for small repairs that inevitably become necessary.

Bottom blacking is a less frequent maintenance cost that most boaters execute every four years. Prices range from £8 to £12 per foot for a full service job, including getting the boat out of the water (with a crane or dry dock) for preparation and re-blacking. Those with more time and patience may plump for a DIY blacking process. You will need to get the boat out of the water and back at a cost of approximately £200, and materials will cost around £100. You may also want to hire equipment such as a pressure washer too.

Blacking

Boat hire companies will usually black their fleet of boats yearly as opposed to the recommended three to four years for private craft. Often they will be happy to claw back some of the costs they incur when hiring a crane by blacking your boat at the same time. This is particularly true if several boats pre-book for blacking at the same time and a bulk discount can sometimes be negotiated. If you contact hire companies late in the season and give plenty of notice it may be possible to cut this cost.

Case studies: Maintenance costs

Becky – *Summer Wine*		Lindsay – *Cerian*	
Total	**£839.88**	**Total**	**£63.57**
2 x chimney coolie hats	£18	Bilge pump	£20
Bilge pump	£33.50	Air filter	£3.50
Flooring	£400	Oil	£6.70
Fenders/chimney	£40	Polish	£9.99
Another chimney	£26.50	Steel wool	£3.99
2 x light fittings	£9.98	Tools	£3.99
Fabric & Foam	£216.90	Cable	£3.50
Woodwork for bed/settee	£95	Rope	£11.90

Maintenance costs

Sarah – *Debonair*

Total	**£1,724**
Electrical works (inc batteries & charger)	£525
Gas pipes/test nipple/labour	£50
Blacking	£370
Gas locker treated/painted	£40
Weed-hatch gasket seal	£40
Oak front cratch boards	£300
Varnish	£12
Fire rope, gland grease & fire blacking	£17
New kitchen taps	£15
2 oak shelves	£100
1 oak work surface	£150
Fire extinguishers (x3)	£105

A professional paint job...

...requires skill, experience and the best quality materials

While the boat is out of the water it is advisable to check sacrificial anodes and replace them if necessary. Purchase and fitting for four anodes will cost around £150 to £200. A hull survey to check the integrity of your steel bottom plate is also an option at this time, particularly if your boat is approaching the age when insurance companies will require one.

Boat painting

For the purposes of this chapter I have concentrated on information from professional boat painters as DIY jobs vary widely in their costs and finish quality.

St Mary's Marina in Rufford near Preston is home to highly regarded boat painter and signwriter Keith Pollitt. He says, 'In boat painting, as with many things, you usually get what you pay for. Our standard service will usually take the boat back to the metalwork so that we can deal with any rust issues below the surface of the current paintwork. We take out all of the windows and remove all roof fittings to be sure that there is no rusty metal beneath, as this can easily spread and ruin a new paint job. From there we assist with and finalise the design, using our experience and skill to guide and advise the boatowner'

Prices for paintwork vary widely depending on which painter you use and how much work is involved in the preparation for the job. At St Mary's, for a routine, well-prepared, multi-coat job you can expect to pay anything from £2,500 for a 40ft boat up to around £5,000 for a 57 footer. 'The amount of prep will define the exact price,' says Keith, 'but regardless of how beaten up

Airbrush boat design

Not all boat painters offer airbrushing, and not all boaters will like it, but for less than £600 you can have almost any design, image or illustration you like on both sides of your boat.

Keith Pollitt at St Mary's
Marina – Rufford

First impressions are important

Resale value

The difference a good-quality paint job can make to an old or tired-looking tub is remarkable and it can have an enormous influence on the value of a boat, something worth thinking about if you intend to sell your boat at any point.

it is, when it comes to us we guarantee to take your breath away when you see the finished piece.'

If a full assault on your boat paintwork is out of your price range, most places will offer an 'economy paint service' that can be considerably cheaper. Either by not removing the windows and fittings or by being less particular about going back to metal, you might be able to get away with less prep and still end up with a great paint job. 'If the paint is just looking faded or tired and there is little or no rust to worry about, we can do a refresher job where we rub down and recoat the boat. This breathes new life into an old paint job and costs considerably less – usually just a grand or two.'

Other random costs

BW facilities key	£6
Anti-vandal (handcuff) key	£5
Windlass	£15
Key float	£3
Sea magnet	£30
Tiller pin	£10
Ecofan	£100

Optional extras

Boating breakdown cover is usually a sensible precaution, particularly for those new to boating, and so it is a cost I always quote to the uninitiated when the question of expenditure arises. The cost will depend on the level of cover required and can range from £80 to £160 a year with the ever-popular River Canal Rescue.

Surfing the Net from your boat is easy nowadays due to 3G mobile technology. Contract deals which include the cost of the USB mobile dongle start at around £10 per month, or if you don't mind paying for the dongle, then a pay-as-you-go deal may suit you better. Top-up vouchers start at around £10 for 1GB of data and are valid for 30 days. Some marinas offer a wireless Internet service at hugely varying costs: I've paid as little as £5 per month and as much as £15 per month. It is worth remembering that both services have their downsides: 3G mobile Internet relies on the strength of a signal, which is variable in different parts of the waterways network, while marina-based wireless services only work while you are moored in your marina.

Conclusion

How long was that piece of string again? Clearly there is no single answer to the question 'how much does it cost?' – there is such an abundance of variables to navigate that boating expenditure can vary wildly. This chapter couldn't possibly be a conclusive list of costs; I'm sure some readers will be paying more and hopefully some will have found fantastic bargains and be paying much less for the products and services I have listed. Boaters are a particularly prudent, resourceful and frugal bunch, but it is worth remembering that 'price' is not always the most important factor when making a purchase of any kind, and that 'value' should always be a consideration too.

SPACE – THE FINAL FRONTIER

There is no getting around the fact that your boat will be smaller than your house, but like most aspects of boating this can be an enormous benefit when viewed from the right perspective. 'Downsizing' one's lifestyle is a process that many people find both refreshing and rewarding, and the transition from house to boat is one of the make-or-break tests for new liveaboard boaters.

The secret is to move aboard with only the bare minimum of possessions and only add more when it becomes absolutely necessary. A good trick is to pack as if for a camping holiday. A suitcase full of clothes and toiletries will suffice for a few weeks until you work out exactly what else you need. Two pieces of cutlery and crockery, a handful of books, a small collection of music, a couple of towels and two changes of bedding will usually suffice, and indeed many liveaboards never feel the need to expand much beyond this list. Moving possessions aboard in stages is the only practical way to do it, and any attempt to move aboard in one go is likely to end up in a stressful and untidy disaster.

Storage aboard

The design of most boats seems to provide plenty of ingenious nooks and crannies for storage, but most of these hidey-holes are not easily accessible. Deckchairs can

Good for the soul and good for the bank balance

Getting rid of the unnecessary junk and clutter you have accumulated is both liberating and rewarding. Just think of all the money you can make by selling your excess gear at car boot sales or on eBay. Depending on how much junk you have, you could earn a decent chunk of money towards the cost of your boat if you start the de-junking process early.

be stored under the bow deck during the winter, but crawling under there for a tool kit in an emergency is not fun. It is worth making a note of the items you use regularly and allocating them a prime storage position that is easily accessible.

If the bed on your boat does not have storage space underneath, it will not be long before you are planning a new bunk. Designing the bed to accommodate baskets or drawers below will give you instant access to everyday items like clothes, bedding and towels. The rest of the space under the bunk is less easily accessed and will probably mean lifting the mattress, so this space is best reserved for items you use rarely such as DIY equipment, camping or outdoor gear and spare bedding for guests. Grouping similar items in containers such as bags and boxes makes it easy to locate and retrieve them in any kind of storage space. A box full of shoes under a seat is more easily found than pulling out each pair individually until you find the ones you want. Packing camping gear and guest bedding inside suitcases and rucksacks frees up lots of space too.

Wardrobe space is another valuable commodity and a ruthless clothing cull is invariably necessary. A 'one in, one out' policy for new clothes will mean less clearing out less often, but it's a tough rule to stick to for some people.

Some boats waste valuable wardrobe space by housing a calorifier water-heating tank there. While these are a great option for leisure boaters or continuous cruisers, most liveaboards will want to have hot water available without the need to run their engine. Removing the calorifier and replacing it with an instantaneous gas water heater will not only free up some space, but also provide a more convenient and cost-effective supply of hot water.

Entertainment

It is notable that many liveaboard boats do not feature a television. Whether this is because boaters are busy with other pursuits or because they have unsubscribed from the banalities of modern life is not clear, but the fact remains true. Flat screen TVs have obvious space-saving advantages, but it is worth considering models with a flip-down screen if your boat design will accommodate it.

Most boats do away with large music sound systems in favour of a car stereo unit, not only to save space but to combat the problem of vibration when under way. However, even car stereo units are becoming obsolete in favour of laptops and MP3 players, thus negating the need to store an expansive collection of CDs.

Outside storage options

Rooftop boxes can be custom built to fit your boat and some boaters even adapt the models intended for use with cars. Both are a good storage option for items such as gardening tools, cleaning products and other low-value boating accoutrements. Similarly the dead space on the back deck of cruiser stern and semi-trad boats can accommodate lockable crates or bench boxes.

Stern hoods are becoming a standard feature on many semi-trad and cruiser stern narrowboats. Although some waterways purists might not appreciate them, the additional covered space is enormously valuable and can be used for many different purposes. Keeping your coal, wood and ash bucket here will minimise clutter and mess inside the boat, and having somewhere to keep muddy boots and wet coats is similarly civilised. Chris Salisbury, from Canvasman, designs, manufactures and fits bespoke covers for all types of boats from narrowboats to seagoing yachts. 'People are surprised at how much practical extra space a canvas hood gives you. Your cratch becomes a useful storage area and we have even seen people use the space under their stern hood as a dining room.'

Ask the Narrowboaters

Question – What is your top space-saving tip?

Becky – *Summer Wine*
Just buy less stuff! I spend a lot less time looking for things I have mislaid now that I have less things and less space to lose them in. Remember, your possessions often end up owning you!

Steve and Eileen – *Rahab*
Buy books from the charity shop, read them and then take them straight back there.

Cratch covers can add extra space to any boat

Every available space is useful

A lockable trunk on a cruiser stern boat

Liveaboard storage tips

- A bin inside a cupboard does not take up floor space.
- Steps make good storage areas with easy access – a tool kit can be stored here, but be sure to have a mini tool kit handy for the inevitable small jobs.
- An over-the-sink drainer is practical and makes use of otherwise dead space.
- Consider using blackout blinds on press studs in corridors with high footfall as curtains and blinds will invariably and frustratingly snag as you walk past them.
- Foldaway chairs for guests can be stored under the gunwales.
- A flip-up table is great for a quick and easy dinner table for mealtimes.
- A 'one in, one out' policy can help to limit the size of your wardrobes and bookshelves, but it is a ruthless and difficult rule to abide by.
- Canvas covers make extra, waterproof internal space for cruiser and semi-trad sterns and the cratches of all types of narrowboat.

Installing canvas hoods for cruiser stern and semi trad boats can be like adding an extra room

- Multi-hangers make good use of small wardrobe spaces.
- Storage containers will save time, space and your sanity.
- Vacuum packs for shrinking and storing clothes that are out of season will free up space.
- A bench seat or crate with a cushion makes a dual-purpose seat and storage area.
- If you haven't used it or worn it in the last 12 months, get rid of it.
- Limit mementos and nostalgia to a maximum of one shoebox.

Container storage under bed

Tony's Towpath Tales

The bane of my existence for my first three years on board was how to cover my windows. Originally I had curtains which hung from a rail, and because the cabin sides of the boat are at an angle, they were tucked behind a retaining bar. This was fine in the wide areas such as my living area and galley, but where the boat narrowed to a passageway I was forever hooking the curtains with my shoulder or getting them caught around whatever I was carrying, leaving them hanging untidily and, occasionally, torn. In an attempt to fix the problem I installed venetian blinds, but these quickly became a dust trap as any horizontal surface does on a boat with a stove. They also bent and snapped easily as my shoulder caught on them when I passed. While roller blinds did not collect dust, they also caught up as I passed by and more than once were torn from their fittings.

Canvas black-out blinds secured with snap caps

Finally, I installed custom-built canvas blinds which attached tightly to the window frame using press stud-type fittings called 'snap caps'. These were set in place each evening and removed each morning, before being rolled and stored beneath my gunwales. Not only do they block out any light, but they also do a fantastic job of keeping in the heat. But the best bit about them is that they fit so tightly that they never get caught up as I walk past. I think every boat should have them!

Roof top box storage

Office filing rules

Office paperwork is one of the most tempting items to hoard. Here's a rundown of how long you need to keep official documents.

- Wage slips – Three months (six years if you are self-employed)
- Tax paperwork – Five years
- Phone bills – One year
- Banking paperwork – Six months
- Receipts – Until guarantee expires
- Self-employment paperwork – Six years

Remember, too, that most paperwork can be avoided by conducting business online. Storage then becomes a file on your laptop – but remember to back up.

5

BOAT TOILETS

Get any group of boaters together and it won't be long until the conversation turns to toilets, as boaters regularly discuss the myriad of toilet types available and their inherent maintenance issues. Whether ordering a new boat or browsing for second-hand vessels, there are several choices to be made when considering a loo.

Pump-out or cassette?

Boat toilets are not like regular land toilets. By their very nature boat toilets cannot be fed directly into the sewers and will need to store their contents for disposal at some later time. This invariably means a second encounter with your bodily waste, and so it is worth considering which toilet system you prefer. Your choice of toilet typically comes down to two options: pump-out or cassette. Cassette toilets have a small removable unit in the base where waste is collected and stored. Pump-out toilets rely on a larger immovable storage (or 'black water') tank, often located beneath a bed or integrally in the bathroom.

Cassette toilets

Cassette toilets are the most popular option for boaters and there are several reasons for this. Firstly they are often the cheapest to install, with basic models costing around £70. These will usually be of plastic construction with smaller-volume cassettes and water reservoirs, and have lever or plunger pump flush systems. While units in this

Ask the Narrowboaters

Q – What can you tell us about your toilet?

John – *Sound of Silence*
When I bought the boat it had a porta potti-style cassette toilet. It would last about a week before it needed emptying. The nearest disposal point is about ten minutes' walk away, which doesn't sound like much, but you try it with a cassette full of ... er ... waste! I even tried transporting it in the basket on the front of a bike before deciding enough was enough.

I recently fitted a dump-through loo which cost me less than £800 for everything I needed to install it, including the wood and other materials. I chose a dump-through because they are foolproof, being such a basic design where very little can go wrong. It is amazing how many boaters rave about cassette toilets and recommend them as the only way to go, but if you look closely, most of these are weekend boaters who don't use their toilets day in and day out. I daresay they would change their tune if they had to carry the cassette up and down the towpath every week of the year.

price range are entirely functional, there are more luxurious models available with features such as electric flush and larger-cassette options. The purchase price is not the only saving to consider when you choose a cassette toilet. Emptying the contents of your cassette into a sanitary disposal point is usually free, whereas there is almost always a charge to pump out a black water tank.

Another important benefit of a cassette toilet lies in the ease with which they can be emptied. A pump-out toilet needs to be taken to a pump-out facility to be emptied. Sometimes this is not possible, for example if you have broken down or if the weather prevents you from moving your boat. If your tank is full and you are nowhere near a pump-out facility then you are in deep doo-doo! Thankfully, with a cassette toilet you can always take Mohammed to the mountain. Removing the cassette for emptying at the nearest facility is much more convenient if your boat is immobile for any reason. Many boaters also keep spare cassettes, just in case they are caught short.

On the downside, cassette toilets are sometimes considered a little uncivilised by the uninitiated. The integral storage unit of cassette toilets means their appearance differs from conventional land loos, leaving guests puzzled and your pan full. Emptying a cassette is an experience that many find objectionable too, and a full cassette is quite a weighty load to carry if the disposal point is any distance away. Ageing and eroded seals in the unit can also cause problems and allow unpleasant leakage, although all seals are relatively cheap and easy to replace. Most cassettes have a ventilation pressure valve which can stick shut if the seal is worn, and this can cause a build-up of gas pressure and a vaporous release when the toilet is next used and flushed.

Pump-out toilets

Those desiring a more conventional-looking toilet will often plump for a pump-out system. These look much more like the toilets you would find in a house and this is often reassuring for those new to boating. Indeed, even some experienced boaters prefer pump-out systems, not only for the aesthetic benefits, but because emptying them is much less of a 'hands-on' experience. Emptying your black water storage tank means a visit to a pump-out facility where there is almost always a charge (usually around £10 to £20). Once paid, emptying involves simply affixing the hose to your storage tank outlet and switching on the machine; the contents are then simply sucked from the tank into either a large tanker unit or directly into the sewers. Many boaters find this to be a much more agreeable process to endure than the emptying of cassettes. Staff in private marinas will sometimes perform the procedure for you (but don't bank on it), whereas BW provides automated facilities which are credited using a prepayment smart card or token and you perform the task yourself.

Pump-out toilet installation costs vary depending on the type of tank and the type of toilet you choose, and there are many variations to choose from. 'Dump-through' systems sit atop a black water holding tank which is usually made of steel. Prices for toilet pans vary from £180 for the most basic to £600 for the most regal model. The pedal flushing systems of most brands are universal across the range, and so paying more money for your toilet buys you a pretty pan rather than any increased reliability.

Vacuum and compressed-air toilets are becoming increasingly popular as they seal off the waste from view once flushed. This disassociation is an attractive benefit for those who prefer a 'home from home' toilet experience. 'Working on this type of toilet isn't too bad either,' says Jo from Snaygill Boats. 'The working bits and moving parts are not attached to the tank or the pan, so if they do break

Justine and Woody – *Frog With A Heart*
We decided upon a cassette toilet primarily as a cost-saving exercise. With two cassettes we can fill one and chuck it in the van before replacing it with the spare. We'd empty the full one at the disposal point on the way to work the next day, saving us having to carry the thing along the towpath. Emptying it didn't worry me too much. You get the occasional splash-back when you are emptying them if you are not careful, but you only do it a couple of times before you learn your lesson.

The only real problem we had was when visitors used the loo. Often they would fill the thing with toilet paper, or fill it with water by flushing it repeatedly. Once we had a visitor use the toilet before we had a chance to replace the cassette, thus causing him to essentially pee through the hole directly onto the floor.

down they can usually be fixed without getting your hands dirty, so to speak.' As with all toilet system benefits there is a price to pay for convenience and these systems are expensive compared with the other available options. A vacuum loo will cost between £1,000 and £1,400 for the vacuum generator and pan combined, whereas a compressed-air system will knock you back £2,000.

As some pump-out toilets can be sited apart from their storage tank it is worth considering that the pipework has the potential to store up to four flushes worth of waste before it arrives at its destination. Michael Punter, from Lee Sanitation, recommends a 'rise and fall' method of routing waste plumbing. 'The waste hose should rise steeply as it leaves the pan before falling gradually into the top of your black water tank. A vacuum or compressed-air flush will easily push waste over the apex of the pipe. It can then flow downhill with gravity into the waste tank, thus avoiding it being stored in the pipework for any period of time. It's also a good idea to keep waste pipes away from hot-water plumbing in order to avoid drying and blockages.'

Costs and convenience are not the only variables to consider when comparing pump-outs with cassettes. Pump-outs are more prone to blocking than their cassette cousins and this can be a monumental problem. All manner of items can disagree with your pump-out toilet, particularly those fitted with a macerator, and visitors are often the unwitting culprits. Disposable nappies, sanitary towels, tampons, condoms and moist toilet tissues are among the countless *objets d'art* removed from blocked pump-out loos. It is easier to say what you *can* put into a pump-out than to list what you can't, and the list is only two items long. The first is anything that has passed through your digestive system, namely faeces and urine. The second item is common or garden toilet tissue. Boaters with delicate derrières should be aware that luxury and quilted toilet tissue does not break down as readily as the more 'value' brands. Macerator toilets have earned a reputation for being prone to blockages, usually due to overenthusiastic tissue usage or plumbing installation problems.

Blockages can also occur when the contents of your tank harden. This can happen if your tank is left for a period of time or if you forego the use of toilet fluids. This

Unusual or troublesome items found in boat toilet tanks

- Five pairs of ladies skimpy underwear
- Paracetamol plastic blister packs
- Sanitary towels and tampons
- Newspaper sheets
- Disposable nappies
- Disinfectant rim blocks

It can cost between £10 and £20 to pump out your toilet tank

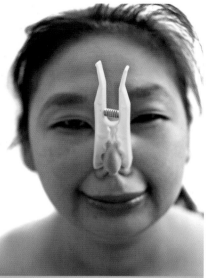

Emptying cassette toilets is an unpleasant task, but you get used to it

allows the contents of your tank to dry out, solidify and collect at the bottom, forming layer after layer of hardened sediment until it eventually reaches and blocks the pump-out hose. Good-quality toilet tissues can exacerbate the problem as the lumpy sediment collects and solidifies to such an extent that it cannot be sucked by the pump-out machinery. With the tank outlet blocked, remedying the situation can be a truly unpleasant experience. While blockages are rare and mostly avoidable, pump-out owners invariably have a story to tell about their toilet tribulations.

There are several ways to address the blockage problem, none of which can be called a joy. Those with a 'dump-through' facility can use a stick or a length of flexible cable to stir the blockage, the aim being to break it up into pieces small enough to pump out. Another way of doing this is to use a pressure washer, but you need to be sure to take care to avoid any splash-back! Caustic soda and sulphuric acid can be used as a last resort, but you should confer with an expert if you decide to go down this road, particularly if your tank is plastic or has no vent system.

Some pump-out toilets have macerator units fitted which grind up any waste before it is stored, with a view to negating blockage problems. While anything which helps avoid a blocked toilet must be applauded, you must be careful not to block the macerator itself as foreign objects can cause the unit to seize. Bear in mind, also, that it is impossible to access black water tanks through a pan with a macerator unit. Most experts consider a tank with a sealable inspection hatch to be a useful insurance in any pump-out set-up.

Finally, eroded seals can be a problem with pump-out toilets too as water from

Bathrooms are usually small but functional

Many styles of toilet are available for your boat

the pan can leak through faulty seals into the storage tank. This can quickly fill a black water tank if the flush water is pumped from the main water supply tank. Again, replacement seals are cheap to buy, and although replacing them on a pump-out system is a little more work, it is entirely doable by anyone with the nose and inclination.

Smell

Storing any amount of bodily waste for any amount of time will generate some smell. There are several ways of dealing with this problem, with the most common remedy being chemical warfare. There are several brands of chemical liquids available for use in both pump-out and cassette systems, most of which are blue in colour and/or name. These formaldehyde-based fluids can be mixed with the water used to flush or used as a solution added directly into the storage tank, but whether you actually like the resulting chemical smell is a matter of taste and tolerance levels.

Flushing dump-through toilets can release the gases that build up inside sealed black water tanks and the odour can be quite offensive. This can be negated by fitting a breather hose from the top of your tank, venting directly outside your boat, and most new boats are fitted with these as a matter of course. Breather hoses allow methane to escape gradually from the tank and not build up in the first place. They should be at least equal to the diameter of the inlet pipes as this allows equal displacement volumes of air and waste when flushing and pumping out.

Water usage

Toilet type	Average water per flush
Dump-through	0.5–1.5 litres
Macerator	2.5 litres
Vacuum	0.5–1.5 litres
Compressed-air	3 litres
Lever-operated sea toilet	4 Litres

Eco-friendly toilets

Boat life is often conducted in close synergy with nature and so it is not surprising that chemical-free eco-friendly toilet systems are becoming increasingly popular. The simplest way to achieve this is by replacing formaldehyde solutions with the more environmentally friendly nitrate and oxygen-based products which essentially speed up the natural decomposition process. These eco-friendly fluids are usually green as opposed to the nasty blue formaldehyde version. Brewer's yeast tablets are also effective in the fight against smells, but be aware that the residues left behind by blue formaldehyde fluids stop both yeast and nitrate fluid systems from working. Boaters wishing to make the transition from formaldehyde to more eco-friendly options usually purchase a replacement cassette, although a period of abstention from chemical usage and some vigorous rinsing may do the trick. It is more difficult to rid black water tanks of formaldehyde as they are tough to rinse and cleanse effectively.

Composting toilets are becoming more popular on boats too, with a variety of systems being available. With some care they can be wonderfully effective in avoiding both smells and disposal problems. In a nutshell they work by allowing oxygen to do its job of drying and composting the waste, and most utilise sawdust as a means of ensuring desiccation. Obviously liquids (such as urine or less solid faeces) can cause problems for the drying process, and if you don't dispose of your wee separately then you'll need to use much more sawdust to keep the compost dry and aerated. Other systems include a heated or fan-dried composting compartment which helps to evaporate the urine more quickly. It could be said that these systems miss the point entirely by using energy to power the units – while doing a poor job of composting to boot.

In reality, most 'composting boaters' don't actually compost their waste on the boat, but transport it ashore to decompose there. The toilets are simple bucket and chuck-it affairs, usually comprising a commode-type throne which is emptied to a compost heap ashore. But many people forget that by forgoing use of the mains sewerage system entirely, composters do not add to the environmental impact of sewerage farms. Along with the reduced chemical impact on the environment, composting toilet owners also save water (by not flushing) and seem to grow the most delicious strawberries!

Sea toilets

Sea toilets were popular on boats before it became illegal to dump sewerage directly into the waterways system. These lever-flushing toilets are still available but must now be pumped into a storage tank. Although some older boats still have overboard pumping sea toilets fitted, the Boat Safety Scheme means that alternative toileting facilities must be available.

Liveaboard loo low-down

Self-pump-out equipment
Self-pump-out kits do exactly what it says on the tin. The kit is either operated manually using a lever or is powered electrically and pumps out the contents of a black water tank into the disposal points used by cassette owners. This usually negates the cost of using traditional pump-out facilities but is a more hands-on approach. A few BW disposal facilities (usually septic tank based) are not free for self-pump-out users as the volumes being discharged are closely managed.

Toilet tissue
Recycled toilet tissue is becoming more robust as manufacturers are increasingly using bonding agents. The people at Lee Sanitation recommend a simple test to see how appropriate your brand of tissue is for boat loo use: put two sheets of toilet tissue into a pint glass of water and stir well. If the tissue breaks up easily then it is boat approved. If it stays in sheets then give it a miss!

Breather hoses
Most of us do not notice any smell from the breather hoses which vent outside our boats, but if you would like to spare the noses of delicate passers-by then you may wish to fit an inline carbon filter.

Tony's Towpath Tales

I've lived aboard my 50ft narrowboat for just over seven years and I cruise the system extensively. I have a dump-through pump-out toilet in which I use a nitrate-based fluid product. I have a ventilation hose fitted to my black water tank which vents methane outside the boat and I pump out about once a month on average. I do also have a cassette-type toilet which lives under my bed for emergencies and this has been used twice in the last seven years. I'm really happy with this set-up and I feel that I have the best of all worlds.

I don't fancy the regular emptying trips that are necessary when using cassette toilets, and considering how regularly I find myself moored in the deepest and darkest recesses of the waterways system I think I'd struggle to find nearby facilities. Besides, as far as I am concerned, once it is out of me, that's the last I want to see of it! I like the concept of composting but I question the inconvenience of having to dispose of urine separately. In my view, if you are regularly disposing of your pee then you may as well use a cassette system. As much as I love strawberries, I can't see myself switching.

Case studies

Toilet trouble 1. *Bob* **– Leeds-Liverpool Canal, West Yorks**
A friend of mine was carrying his full cassette to be emptied one summer afternoon when he slipped and fell on the towpath. As the cassette hit the floor it burst open, covering him with the contents, which was unpleasant enough. However, his sympathies lay with the guests on the restaurant boat moored directly next to the incident who were attempting to enjoy an al fresco lunch.

Toilet trouble 2. *Ruben* **– Erewash Canal, Derbyshire**
My parents enjoyed occasional days out on my boat in the summer but my mum was particularly wary of my dump-through pump-out loo. They came to visit one weekend and on arrival my mum rushed to use the loo after the long journey from London. I was a little worried when she called my dad for help, and even more so when I found out why. Somehow my mother had managed to drop her car keys into the pan and flush them into the poo tank. I was left to retrieve them while they retired to a nearby pub for lunch.

THE ART OF BOATING

Most of the UK's waterways are managed and maintained by three separate bodies. Canals are predominantly the responsibility of British Waterways, rivers fall under the care of the Environment Agency and the rivers and lakes of the Norfolk and Suffolk Broads are governed by the Broads Authority. It is important to familiarise yourself with the rules and guidelines of each organisation if you are to be travelling within their jurisdiction as there are some notable variations. However, the guidelines in this chapter will equip you with most of the information you will need for safe and happy boating wherever you may roam.

When passing boats coming towards you, the boats should ideally pass port (left) side to port side, unless conditions dictate otherwise. It is good practice to slow down here too, as excessive speed will cause the boats to come together, reducing control of your boat and increasing the need to take evasive action. A weaving (or breaking) wash is usually the sign of a poor helmsman. Look out particularly for approaching boats at bridges and blind bends; with such a reduced line of sight you need to slow down well in advance. Speeding up in an attempt to beat the other boat through the bridge is a recipe for disaster, especially if the other helmsman has the same idea. The result could be a collision or cause both boats to get stuck in the bridge hole, both of which can compromise safety and your bank balance.

Setting-off checklist

It is easy to get caught up in the excitement when preparing for a day out on your boat. If you are anything like me you'll be itching to cast off those ropes and get going, but like all things boating, it is usually a mistake to rush. Here's a handy checklist of things to remember before setting off. I'm so forgetful I have a copy pinned next to my engine ignition, just in case!

- Clear the roof of obstacles such as bicycles, plant pots and the like. They can be trip hazards when walking on the roof and may also foul low bridges, particularly if water levels are high.
- Ensure all safety equipment, including lifejackets, life rings and throwing ropes, is on board and to hand.
- Raise your fenders to avoid drag and to avoid losing them. They can also be hazardous in locks should they become entangled.
- Have your mooring pins and mallet to hand ready for when you need to moor.
- Check your headlight and horn, particularly if you are heading for a tunnel.
- Check engine coolant and oil levels before setting off as this cannot be done once the engine is hot.
- Is your midline handy near your tiller, or have you left it coiled nicely at the centre of your boat?
- A pole and hook should be within reach on your roof. An anchor with a rope and chain of appropriate length is necessary if cruising on rivers, and a gangplank is useful too.

Useful items

- Windlass
- Handcuff key
- Waterproofs
- Binoculars
- Snacks/drinks
- First-aid kit
- BW key
- Waterways map
- Hat/gloves/scarf
- Sunglasses/sunblock
- Umbrella

Utilities checklist

- Toilet capacity
- Coal/wood/firelighters
- Water
- Gas

Slow down to tickover speeds when passing moored boats

- Make sure your tiller and pin are found and affixed before casting off your mooring ropes.
- Make sure you have disconnected your electricity landline cable.
- Tighten the stern gland greaser at the end of each cruise and ensure the bilge pump has been doing its job.
- Stock your larder before setting off; at least have tea- and coffee-making necessities along with the ingredients for tomorrow's breakfast. A disposable barbecue is a canny standby, and powdered milk will tide you over until the next stop.
- Secure any delicate or precarious breakables on board.
- If you have pets on board ensure you have their needs catered for. This may include a doggy lifejacket but will certainly include their food. You may wish to pack their favourite toy too.

Running aground

It is common to run aground near the edges of the waterway, particularly when attempting to moor. The best way to get off the ground is by going back the way you came. By attempting to force your way onward you will probably only become more stuck. Reversing off is usually sufficient, but reducing the weight on board by depositing a passenger onto the bank will often help too.

Quote

'It is good to have an end to journey towards, but it is the journey that matters in the end.'
(Ursula K Le Guin – American author)

As with driving, the safety and consideration of one's passengers are the primary focus of a good helmsman. While there is no substitute for practice and experience, knowing the basics of boating technique and etiquette will give you a head start. From boat handling to best practice, there are plenty of sources of useful information. *The Boater's Handbook* and its accompanying DVD from British Waterways and the Environment Agency offer a wealth of safety and handling advice, while www.considerateboater.com talks you through the dos and don'ts of boating etiquette, and many companies offer practical helmsman courses. 'Boating headaches are usually due to a lack of boating experience and know-how, rather than attitude,' says Steve Vaughan from ConsiderateBoater.com. 'A little research and reading can help boaters avoid most problems until they get a bit of boating experience under their belt.'

When under way

The most frequent cause of frustration among boaters is speed, particularly when passing moored boats. While a well-moored boat will withstand all but the most discourteous of passing traffic, slowing down to a slow crawl is the most considerate course of action. Speed is a relative concept and what might appear to be adequately slow to a boat on the move might seem too fast to a moored boater. A sure-fire way to ensure you are travelling slowly enough is to go as slow as your boat possibly can. Put your engine in neutral before adding just enough revs to get the propeller moving. Only then can you be certain that you are going slowly, not just slow*er*. Slowing down can be frustrating if you need to pass long

Anglers

Anglers and boaters invariably get in each others' way and the only way to avoid conflict is to be as courteous as possible. Slow down as you approach them and do not increase your revs until you are well past their position. Stick to the centre of the navigation and, if the angler is landing a big fish, stop your boat and watch the proceedings. Look out for fishing competition notices when mooring up or you could get an early wake-up call.

Hire boat fleet

lines of moored boats, but it should be remembered that waterways life is never fast. In windy conditions it may be necessary to keep a little speed up, but use only the minimum necessary.

With a 4mph speed limit, overtaking is rarely necessary and should only be attempted when both helmsmen are aware of and understand the manoeuvre being undertaken. Choose a straight, wide piece of water and give clear hand signals. The passing boat should ideally pass on the port side of the slower vessel and should move as slowly as possible but as quickly as necessary.

Boat hirers

Hirers are not pirates but many private boatowners have a holier-than-thou attitude towards them. While it is true that most hirers will not have the experience and expertise of a seasoned boater, it is worth remembering that we were in exactly the same position once upon a time and many of us were bitten by the boating bug through hiring. 'If it wasn't for hire boats then the waterways as we know them would not exist,' Steve Vaughan of ConsiderateBoater.com reminds us.

Hire companies work hard to ensure that their customers have enough tuition to manage the boat, but an hour of coaching cannot make an expert boater. Few hirers will be purposely discourteous but novices are going to make mistakes. Often a hirer will welcome some considered and friendly advice, but don't be put out if they don't want it. Few of us enjoy our errors being highlighted.

Hire boats ready to go

Hire state of consciousness

Jo – Snaygill Boats

It usually takes a few days for our boat hirers to settle in to the boating mindset. If we are going to get calls about running out of water or battery life problems, we know it will be in the first week of the hire period. After that time they start to regulate their usage and consumption and generally ease back and start enjoying boat life. After the hire is over they are so relaxed that we often see them pull out of the car park at a very sedate pace.

Locks, swing bridges and tunnels

Sharing lock and swing bridge labour is a great way to meet your fellow boaters and is one of the most pleasurable aspects of living aboard. While there are no hard and fast rules, there is a suggested code of conduct which aids safety and encourages goodwill. Be sure to wait your turn if there is a queue, and be aware that boats that appear to be moored may in fact be waiting in line. Always check for other approaching boats before moving locks or bridges to make more efficient use of water and reduce waiting time for road traffic. Make sure your boat crew does their fair share of the workload rather than sitting in the cabin drinking tea. Look for approaching boats again before you close the bridge or the lock gates. When sharing locks it is important to err on the side of caution; open paddles slowly and confer with the other boat's crew to let them know what you are doing.

Mooring

Mooring durations and restrictions are discussed in detail in another part of this book, but considerate mooring practices deserve a mention here too. Mooring next to any structure, such as bridges, locks, tunnels, bends, winding holes, water points or sanitary stations, can cause problems and is sometimes dangerous. Stopping at these places should be restricted to the minimum amount of time you need to use the facilities, and in the case of bends and winding holes, not at all. If you decide to moor anywhere near one of these features, be sure to leave more than enough space for boats

Five Rise Locks on the Leeds and Liverpool canal in Bingley

Slow down for bridges and tunnels

Hold tight

Keep a tight hold on the windlass when using locks and always use the safety catches. Spinning windlasses can cause serious injury.

to use the facilities without needing to make delicate or difficult manoeuvres.

Boaters will often choose a mooring on a quiet bit of towpath with a view to avoiding the busy visitor moorings nearby, and while there is no rule that says you cannot moor there too, choosing a spot a short distance away is the polite thing to do. Mooring on the non-towpath side (offside) is often impossible and not usually recommended. Offside land is usually private and a haven to flora and fauna which can be disturbed by mooring boats. Think of other nearby humans too, particularly if mooring in residential areas, and keep noise to a minimum; this includes engine running, music and noisy barbecue parties. BW rules state that engines must not be running between 8pm and 8am.

Ten boating etiquette tips

1   Cruising a frozen canal is possible, but be aware that fragile GRP and wooden boats can be damaged by large sheets of moving ice.
2   When setting off, be sure to check for approaching boats. It is easy to get caught up in the pre-cruise concentrated excitement and not notice that you are about to cast off into the path of an oncoming vessel.
3   Give a long toot of your horn when approaching bridges and blind bends. Short toots can be mistaken for car horns. Using your horn to signal to an oncoming boater in plain view is not ideal as it could be misinterpreted. Much better to flash your headlight and use clear hand signals.
4   Cyclists, anglers, walkers and other boaters will all appreciate a smile and a wave as you pass, and as this is one of the most pleasurable aspects of boating, not doing so is almost unforgivable.
5   Always knock and ask before boarding someone else's boat. Stepping aboard uninvited is usually considered impolite.
6   Use hi-vis tape or white plastic bags to highlight mooring pins, and keep the towpath next to your boat clear of other trip hazards.
7   Be ready to help at locks and bridges, even if you are cruising single-handed. Be mindful that the skipper of the boat might want to do things differently or more slowly than you might be accustomed to. Not everyone is an expert boater.
8   Try to leave space for other boats to moor at popular visitor moorings. This may mean shuffling along a few feet as boats arrive and leave.
9   Be aware that fallen dead wood is a valuable ecological commodity, since it is home or food for a wealth of flora and fauna. Localised collecting near marinas or popular mooring points can desecrate an area in a very short time. Most boaters consider it acceptable to collect dead wood that can be reached from the towpath; everything else belongs to Mother Nature.
10 Moorings with facilities for the disabled are rare, so stay off these unless you are entitled. There is usually only a small sign to highlight this type of mooring, so keep a keen eye when mooring up.
    For more information see www.considerateboater.com.

River boating

Navigating rivers presents more risk than simple canal cruising, particularly if the river is tidal or has a strong current. Seemingly routine manoeuvres such as boating under bridges, entering and leaving locks and even mooring up are much more difficult in a fast-flowing current, and inexperienced boaters should seek guidance. Getting it wrong on a river can have far greater consequences for both your boat and those aboard.

    Proper planning is important. Speak to boaters with experience of the river you

Canalside bustle. Photo by Chris Beesley

River insurance

Make sure that you and your boat are insured to travel on tidal waterways. Some policies specifically exclude this.

will be cruising and ask their advice about the specific idiosyncrasies of that river. Local lock-keepers are invaluable here too and most can guide you around the major hazards and offer specific navigational advice. The lock-keepers will tell you when it is safe to travel, taking into account the currents and tides, and only a fool would ignore their guidance.

Make sure that you have the right safety equipment on board and that your crew know what to do and how to use it, should the need arise. In a deep and fast-flowing river, even the strongest swimmer is in danger if they fall overboard. Lifejackets must always be worn and the boat should be equipped with throwing ropes and life rings kept in easy reach. An anchor is another must-have item. Often this is the only way to bring a stricken boat to a safe stop if the engine fails for whatever reason. A VHS radio is invaluable for communication with lock-keepers and the large commercial vessels that are commonly found on rivers. Coming across one of these large craft laden with cargo is daunting to say the least, so it's

Rule 1 – Two boats are better than one

Always travel in tandem with another boat when navigating rivers. Most problems are dealt with much more easily if another boat is there to help or tow you to safety.

Ask the Narrowboaters

Q – Do you have any river-cruising tips?

Steve and Eileen – *Rahab*
We were stuck on a flooded river for a couple of weeks when the water level was so high that the locks onto the canal were closed. As the water rose it became clear that we were at risk of being washed onto the bank. In the end we used the bargepole and gangplank to wedge between the boat and the bank to keep us on the river, ready for when the water level dropped. It was quite an adventure wading through 3ft of water to get to the boat!

best to be prepared for them and ensure that they are prepared to meet you.

River mooring

River moorings need careful consideration as a pleasant high-tide mooring spot can become a steep mudbank with alarming speed. If you are simply passing through as part of your journey you will find floating pontoons at conveniently spaced intervals. These rise and fall with the tide and are usually positioned near road bridges or other branches of the waterways system. The lock-keepers stationed at tidal rivers will monitor your position as you cruise through their patch, so it is important to notify them if you intend to stop at a floating pontoon en route.

Mooring at the pontoons on tidal rivers is not as easy as mooring on a canal. The tide and the current must be considered, as each presents a challenge. Approaching a pontoon mooring *with* a fast-flowing tide or current is a dangerous undertaking. There is a significant risk of losing control of your vessel if the current is strong enough to claim your boat as you attempt to step ashore, not to mention the risk of falling in. The best way is to approach the mooring *against* the current by continuing slightly past the pontoon before turning your boat around and heading back. This makes for a much slower and more controlled approach as your engine counteracts the direction and force of the current.

It is possible to moor at bankside if the proper facilities are in place, but these are not usually available for visiting boats. Many permanent riverside moorers use a floating pontoon secured to a hinged metal structure which rises and falls with the tide. These simple contraptions are often made from scaffolding poles and work exceedingly well. Some even have a secure gated access point installed.

The rising and falling water level of both rivers and the canals that are fed from them has caught many boaters unawares. Some seemingly non-tidal waterways can rise and fall alarmingly, leaving a tightly moored boat bound or suspended from its ropes at an unnerving angle. Ask advice from local boaters or lock-keepers regarding the eccentricities of the waterway, and be sure to take account of rising and falling water levels.

River locks

Leaving the river via a lock requires careful planning too. A fast-flowing current can thwart an unprepared boater, dashing your boat against the lock wall as you enter, or causing you to overshoot the entrance to the lock completely. When approaching *with* the tide you should begin your approach turn into the lock very early and be ready to use your engine in short, sharp bursts as you enter the lock. When entering a lock *against* the tide you should advance slightly past the lock entrance before turning in, since the current will drag you back the way you came as your boat turns broadside. Follow advice from the lock-keeper closely as they know their lock and the river flow well and have completed the manoeuvre many times before.

It may seem that river cruising is a risky business and perhaps well avoided, but like most risky endeavours there are significant rewards to be had in return. Access to many sections of the waterways network is only possible via a river stretch, and besides, river cruising is exciting and awe-inspiring with its grand scale and new experiences. It might be worth hiring an experienced skipper to coach you as you navigate a river cruise, or perhaps joining another experienced boater on their next river jaunt. There is much to learn and safety should be your first consideration, but river boating is a fantastic experience if it is done correctly.

Ask the Narrowboaters

Q – Is boating different for liveaboards?

Steve and Eileen – *Rahab*
Not really, but liveaboards often have more time to stop and chat with people. It is one of the things we noticed when we moved aboard, that spending a few days or weeks in a single spot seems to give you a better taste for the area. You meet the same people for a few days and before you know it they are stopping to chat and drinking tea with you. We have met some lovely folk and have stayed in touch with quite a few of them.

John – *Sound of Silence*
Only in the sense that your boat is your home. Whilst I don't suppose any boater is inclined to take risks, I know that it is always in the back of my mind that if something goes wrong then I could lose my home and my belongings.

Tony's Towpath Tales

Single-handed boating

It was still pleasantly warm as I rocked gently in my hammock after a long day on the cut. The claret-red backdrop of sky was gatecrashed by occasional swooping bats as they hunted for their supper, while fat silver carp jumped and flipped in the water. The sun was finally dipping below the horizon of hills and I grinned again as I looked around, pleased with myself for finding such a beautiful and serene mooring. My journey would begin again tomorrow and this place would become another memory of a great day on the cut. But for a few hours it was mine to enjoy selfishly, all to myself.

I've lived aboard my 50ft narrowboat for over seven years and I've explored a fair chunk of the network in that time. I'll often have at least one crew on board to help with locks and tea-making duties and the like, but I always look forward to those days when I can cruise alone. Perhaps it is because our modern world is so full of continual chatter and communication that we don't often get a chance to enjoy being by ourselves. Whatever the reason, I look forward to those long stretches of canal when I can cruise along in my own little world of quiet, uninterrupted solitude.

Summertime

During the summer months there are plenty of other boaters, fishermen and pedestrians around to punctuate my day, and for the most part these are a welcome distraction. While I am perfectly able to negotiate locks and moving bridges single-handed, the opportunity to shoot the breeze with other boaters is one of the greatest pleasures of life on the cut, despite our conversations being executed in series, and cut short when the lock gates open to let us out for the next round of tillering.

I always make a point of hopping ashore with a windlass so that I can do my fair share of the work, but more often than not there are enough hands ashore and I'm encouraged to stay aboard. I must admit I do feel quite lazy, perched at the tiller, chatting with the other skipper while their industrious crew scurry across the locks. I always keep a supply of biscuits handy to share by way of a thank you.

Locks and moving bridges

Locks and moving bridges can be wearisome when cruising alone. As a remedy I have found the best approach is to dispense with the idea

Single-handed boating is a liberating experience. Photo by Chris Beesley

of speed and efficiency, and instead embrace the slow and methodical nature of the process. Indeed, I find that almost every part of boat life is more pleasurable if one adopts this philosophy. At locks I use my binoculars on the approach to select a suitable mooring point before sauntering up to the towpath at a slow tickover. I'll moor loosely, take a leisurely look around and perhaps collect some unsightly litter before preparing the lock and bringing the boat in at a crawling pace.

It seems that the deeper the lock, the more nervous I become, particularly if using the lock ladder to board and alight. My boat always seems a little forlorn and vulnerable when left on its own at the bottom of a lock, and I'm always eager to get back aboard. Despite this impatience, I feel entirely more comfortable and confident if I use only the paddles on my side of the lock, dispensing entirely with the need to rush across the gate. Admittedly this is a time-consuming option, but I'm happy to compromise speed for serenity. As I step aboard and pull away I say a little thank you to the Waterways gods for allowing me safe passage through another lock, single-handed.

Executing swing bridges is an exercise in science, skill and luck in equal proportion. There are many variables to consider and even a simple moment of distraction can prove troublesome. I am always wary of windows and cratch covers becoming impaled on the corner of the bridge, which always seems to swing closed a little, no matter how stiff it was to open. The wind is no friend of mine either and seems to conspire against me consistently when negotiating a tricky swing bridge. Again, I find that the answer to swing bridge stress is a slow, considered approach where I resign myself to the fact that it will never go perfectly according to plan and that life would be boring if everything did. The tribulations of single-handed swing bridging are part of the ever-present trials of boat life, and one must either get on with it or give up. I do always feel a little smug and accomplished when I'm safely back on board and the sight of the bridge is fading into the distance behind me.

Safety

Sir Francis Younghusband once said, 'Experience teaches much, and teaches it sharply,' and thankfully my experiences of mishaps have been few and the consequences minor. Relishing the carefree, idyllic life on the waterways alone must be contrasted with a strict and concentrated approach to safety, particularly one's own. It is foolish to risk personal injury in an attempt to save a window or 'cilled' stern gear, particularly as incidents involving single-handed boaters may go unnoticed for hours. Despite my own cautiously focused approach, there have been occasional near misses where only my strong grip on the boat or lock ladder has saved me after a slip. I'm convinced enough of the risks to always wear a self-inflating lifejacket when locking single-handed. Despite having not yet fallen into a lock I can't help calculating the increasing odds of doing so each time I repeat the process. Perhaps one day my luck will fail and my number will come up. On that day I'll be wearing a lifejacket with a waterproof mobile phone and a whistle in the pocket.

Winter

If pushed to make a choice I would grudgingly admit that I prefer boating in the warm summer months, but grudgingly for sure, as winter cruising has its own magical charm. I love frosty mornings with branches sleeved in a silver sheen, smoke unfolding from my chimney and not a soul in the world to be seen. True connoisseurs of solitude will relish these cold, crisp months when one can cruise for days without passing another moving boat, enjoying the fantasy that the waterways were yours to own.

During the winter, boating comes into sharp focus as every activity and manoeuvre becomes more acute. My fingers are crossed, with prayers and curses each morning, as I attempt to start my decrepit old engine that really should have been serviced during the comfortable summer months. I cling to the hope of finding a coal merchant to replenish my dwindling supplies; and another bottle of gas would stop me fretting too.

Boating during the winter is tough but rewarding

Icy lock beams and ladders concentrate my attention, as do the freezing cold hand rails of my boat. I'm always amused when my wet ropes from yesterday are frozen in coils or straight like dowelling rods by last night's freeze. All of these musings trip through my mind repeatedly during the day, and without a crew to confer with the responsibility of dealing with them is entirely mine. Some may consider such tribulations to be a bind, but for me they are tests which give me a sense of accomplishment and pride once each is safely overcome.

Single-handed cruising is not easy and usually requires adaptations in both technique and attitude. But for those with sufficient supplies of brains and brawn, cruising the waterways alone can be a rewarding and often meditative enterprise, despite the logistical conundrums presented by the various designs of locks and bridges. Repetition is the mother of all skill and many single-handed boaters will claim to be at least as efficient as crewed vessels.

But the real joy of single-handed cruising lies not in the speed at which one can negotiate a lock, or ease with which one masters a swing bridge, but in the uninterrupted and serene enjoyment of the waterways and one's boat. I love spending time alone and aboard and I would highly recommend the experience. But I don't think I can say with any sincerity that I have ever truly cruised alone. In reality, it has always been a team effort: me, and my boat.

We make a great team and she's never let me down.

Single-handed cruising tips

Ladders are a relatively recent addition to the historic structures of locks and were introduced as a safety escape feature, rather than as an aid to boating. Although many single-handers find the ladders useful, some consider them unnecessary, preferring instead to haul their boat in and out of the lock using ropes. This bow-hauling method works fine in most cases, although those locks with bridges at their entrance or exit can prove problematic. For boaters with the necessary co-ordination, one answer is to stand atop the bridge and nimbly flick the rope beneath before catching the end at the other side. For those of us lacking in this skill, using the lock ladder is arguably a more efficient method, as long as one is conscious of the ever-present slip hazard.

One of the greatest dangers when negotiating a lock alone comes in the form of friendly help. Despite their best intentions, enthusiastic assistance from inexperienced or distracted windlass wielders can create problems and things can go wrong surprisingly quickly. Don't be afraid to decline help as most boaters will understand that everyone has their own way of doing things. Explain that you have a 'system' and that it is hard to break the habit. Of course, if you are sharing a lock with another boat and their crew, it is everyone's responsibility to stay alert to danger. By all means enjoy the company while you can, but keep a watchful eye on proceedings to ensure everyone stays safe and afloat.

A centre rope is your greatest friend when boating alone. Ensure the end of the rope is within reach of your position at the tiller, ready for when you need to step ashore. In most situations you can use the centre rope alone to moor to the bank while preparing a lock, before using a bow rope to haul the boat in when the lock is ready. Use the centre rope again to maintain a good position in the lock, taking in or letting out slack when necessary. Be especially careful when locking down, as boats can easily be hung up if a rope is tied to a bollard. It does also help to have a centre rope on each side of the boat if possible as this avoids the need to flick the rope over chimneys and other roof clutter when the need arises.

'Thumblining' is an intricate method through which a lock gate is opened and closed without disembarking by using ropes, and was routinely used by working boats towing a cargo butty. The process is unfortunately now almost extinct, and indeed modern lock restoration work has tended to dispose of a mandatory small pin which protruded near the top lock, making thumblining impossible.

Lift bridges and swing bridges rely on the use of long ropes, convenient landing points and accurate boat manoeuvring, often supplemented by no little agility and climbing skill. They should always be approached slowly and methodically, and it is useful to practise the process when you have a crew to step in with help should motorists become impatient. Be aware that some electrically operated bridges have a timer to delay overfrequent usage, or a locking period to prohibit being used at peak road traffic times.

A midline rope is vital for single handed boaters

It is often asked why most swing bridges leave single-handed skippers on the other side of the cut from their moored boat. It is, in fact, a historical feature left over from the time when boats were pulled by horses along the towpath. An open bridge on the towpath side would ensnare the rope between horse and boat, whereas boat crews could easily negotiate bridges on the offside with no risk of entanglement. It could be argued that bridges should be renovated to accommodate our modern engine-driven boating needs, but the heritage of our waterways should perhaps not be discarded so readily. I find the anomalies and ambiguity to be a rather endearing feature of boating and hope that the heritage of our inland waterways is preserved as closely as possible, even if the resulting tricky swing bridges make me curse occasionally.

Who needs a crew?

7

WORKING NINE TO FIVE?

While working and boating are not mutually exclusive, they rarely seem to fit together neatly. Finding a suitable mooring location and the transient nature of boating can both be difficult for those who work in one place. Even those who work for themselves can encounter communication and logistical challenges. However, most of the problems can be overcome with a little ingenuity, planning, hard work and good luck. The solution may be a radical one, but boaters are generally a resourceful bunch and most would not allow a small inconvenience such as a job to stand in the way of their liveaboard dream.

Work and the continuous cruiser

Juggling a regular job with continuous cruising is very difficult and so most employed liveaboards have a permanent mooring. Waterways regulations state that continuous cruisers must move to a new district at least every two weeks, and hopping back and forth to stay near your workplace will soon attract the attention of the local moorings officer and disapproving fellow boaters.

There are many other inconveniences too. Retrieving your car each time you cruise to a new location can be a logistical nightmare, and commuting by public transport is complicated or impossible under continuous-cruising conditions. It can also be difficult to find enough time to run the engine to charge leisure batteries, and so power consumption often becomes critical and rationed.

Finding the right mooring close to your chosen work will mean an easy commute by bike

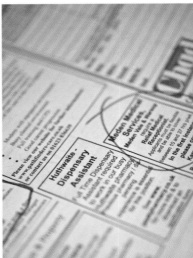

Living aboard can change your work/life balance

Recruitment agencies offer a limited and intermittent solution for some liveaboard continuous cruisers. Offering your services to the agencies in each new district you moor can secure a temporary income until you move on, but most available agency work assignments are poorly paid unless you have a valuable skill that is in demand, and the proximity of your boat will still depend on mooring duration regulations. Consider, too, that this type of itinerant employment is unlikely to deliver a constant flow of work, particularly during times of economic downturn, although intermittent work is often all the liveaboard needs if their lifestyle is sufficiently frugal.

While intermittent employment is an option, this type of lifestyle is hardly convenient or stress-free. Most continuous cruisers are self-employed or have another means of income, and most of those who start off as salaried nine-to-five workers soon tire of it, eventually giving up either their job, their boat or their continuous-cruising attempts.

Working from a permanent mooring

Finding a mooring that is near enough to your place of work will often mean making a compromise. Your daily commute is the most likely sacrifice as you will probably need to balance the mooring location and facilities against the proximity to your work. That said, the availability of local moorings are likely to dictate your options to you. Be sure to read the moorings chapter of this book closely.

Registering with local recruitment agencies may secure some temporary work before you move on again

Eileen would rather be boating!

Having a permanent mooring need not inhibit the boater's tendency to roam, but having a regular job certainly seems to. The convenience of a permanent mooring, particularly one with good facilities, is hard to give up, and once again the boater must balance the desire to use their boat as it was intended against the necessity of earning a living.

Determined liveaboard boaters will often make radical changes in order to live the lifestyle to which they aspire, and the method of earning a living is usually high on the list of changes to be made. Many new liveaboards seem to undergo a career change as they covet a less stressful life or because their current employment does not accommodate a boating lifestyle. Necessity being the mother of all invention, boaters with enough courage and determination will usually find a means to achieve their goal and find a happy compromise.

The usual boating-specific challenges can complicate matters for liveaboards who work from home or work for themselves. Phone signal, address issues, Internet connection, mail and courier deliveries and even the limited space on board can each be a headache, but innovative and determined boaters will either find a solution, or create one.

Renting out your boat

While on a frugality and downsizing mission, people will usually make radical changes to their lifestyle. For new boaters looking for innovative ways to save and earn more money, hiring and renting out their boat may appear to be a good way to capitalise on their asset. It might seem like a good idea, but in reality this type of commerce only makes sense for those running a fleet of boats. Insurance and Boat Safety requirements are the main financial factors to consider and are imperative, of course, since the safety of your boat and that of the hirers or tenants is vitally important. Supplying proper training and instruction on boat handling and facilities is an art, and ongoing support when things go wrong is vital. Breakages, wear and tear and theft must all be factored in to any business plan involving boat hire, making the venture viable only for larger-scale operations. Unofficial hiring and renting does happen, but the potential for it turning into a nightmare is enormous.

Tony's Towpath Tales

Occupation – freelance writer
I chose my boat specifically because it had space for an office. After ripping out a bunk I installed a small desk, a filing cabinet and some bookshelves and I now run my freelance writing career from this tiny 6ft x 4ft office space. Most of my work can be conducted via email and by phone, and only rarely are meetings or interviews held aboard my boat. (When they do occur, the interviewee is invariably enthralled.) I hire cars when I need them and my post is delivered to the local sorting office for collection.

A frugal boating lifestyle was very important in the early years of building my writing career as I could not have managed the expenses of running a house on my initially meagre income. The boat was instrumental in helping me to make the leap to be a full-time writer and the career suits my boating lifestyle. I can travel around the waterways network and moor where I like. I have moved around quite a lot, but I do settle at permanent moorings, as having water and power on tap is very convenient.

Darren: *Dunster*

You'll often find musicians living aboard

Ask the Narrowboaters

Q – How does living aboard affect your work?

**Darren – *Dunster*
Occupation – musician**
When I lived in a house I had a much bigger studio and more equipment and more instruments. Most of these were sold when I moved aboard as there wasn't enough space. I did stash some of my kit at a friend's recording studio and inevitably these got used by other artists recording there. In return I get to use the studio equipment for free, so I haven't really lost out at all, and it is nice to share resources around within our profession.

Being on a boat hasn't stopped me from making music for a living despite the constraints. I think that if you have the right attitude you can find a way around most things if you really want to, and the pros definitely outweigh the cons. Sometimes we move the boat closer to where we are playing a gig if the venue is near a nice place on the canal. Boat life is also a great way for a musician to live: all that outdoors and travel and relaxation is just the right environment for creativity to flourish.

Steve and Eileen – *Rahab*
Occupation – photographer and teacher respectively

Living on a boat has not had much impact on our work lives at all. We both earn a living teaching part-time and Steve also runs a photography business. We both bring work back home to the boat but it is the type of work that can easily be done on a laptop whilst sat on the sofa. We both have a car, so commuting is easy, and when we are out and about on the boat it is not much of a problem to use public transport.

We have worked around a few small challenges. For example, a 45ft boat does not leave much room for the amount of photography kit that Steve apparently needs, so we tend to store some of that stuff elsewhere. Steve also holds photography courses at a hired venue, whereas if we lived in a house he could probably host it there.

We both chose to work part-time because we didn't want to sell our souls to a lifestyle that revolved around work and money. We earn less but we have more fun and free time, which fits in nicely with our relaxed boating lifestyle and ethos. In fact, Steve turned down some lucrative work just recently as it would have meant long days and a long commute. It just didn't seem worth the stress. In an ideal world we would like to do more boating

Steve: *Rahab*

and see more of the network, but we have found a happy balance between that ideal and the need to earn a living.

Sandra and Bob – *All Things Spanish*
Occupation – waterways traders

My great-great-grandfather was a boatman, so the idea to live aboard came before the intention to run a business from a boat. Although we are supposed to be retired we couldn't stand the idea of sitting around twiddling our thumbs all day. We used to live in Tenerife and still rent out cottages there, so the idea to sell Spanish delicatessen produce from the boat stemmed

Sandra: *All Things Spanish*

from here. We sell refreshments, tea, coffee, cakes and the like along with Spanish products such as cheeses, spices and other cooking ingredients.

We spoke to our local BW business manager who helped with the administration and official stuff. We pay approximately 10% more for our waterways licence and our insurance is around 25% more expensive to cover public liability. We also had an environmental health inspection and they issue a certificate once it is passed.

Our decision to live aboard is predominantly a lifestyle choice and the business sits nicely alongside. We cruise the local network visiting spots we feel likely to be good for business, keeping meticulous notes. Running a fridge and a freezer on board means we need to run the engine for a good few hours to keep the batteries charged. The English weather is a big consideration for a business such as ours too, but we don't mind it too much. It is nice to be back in England because it has such nice countryside.

HOME COMFORTS

Imagine the scene ... It is January and the evenings are cold and dark by six o'clock. You arrive home late from work, and after taking off your wet coat and your muddy boots you start to build a fire, only to find that your coal scuttle is empty. Thankfully you have adequate supplies stacked neatly beside your boat, but to refill your scuttle means going outside again, into the wind and the rain.

Ten minutes later you remove your coat and boots for the second time and begin to build the fire. In half an hour your boat should be comfortably warm, but until then, only a steaming mug of tea will help. You fill the kettle and light the hob before filling the sink with soapy water. It's time to tackle last night's dishes, but halfway through filling, the tap begins to splutter – a sure sign that your water tank is about to run dry. Now you have a dilemma. Do you postpone the dishes and tomorrow morning's shower, or do you brave the weather once again and fill your tank? Resignedly you don your boots and coat once again and head out into the rain with your hosepipe.

By the time you get back inside the roaring stove has warmed your boat nicely and you look forward to a well-earned cup of tea. But surely the kettle should be boiling by now? With a glance towards the hob you realise that your gas bottle has run out. It is small consolation that it did so now and not in the morning when you were in the shower covered in soap and running late for work. And at least your batteries are not flat ... yet.

Welcome to boat life, albeit in a condensed form. You would be very unlucky (or disorganised) indeed for all of these frustrations to afflict you in a single night, but afflict you they will, at almost predictably regular intervals. This is the major difference between life afloat and living in a house. In a house, your home comforts and utilities are available at the flick of a switch, on tap and seemingly infinite. On a boat, your supply of these consumable resources will run out eventually. Perhaps this is why green living is popular in the boating community, as the analogy lends itself easily to the environmentalist's cause. Peter Underwood writes about living aboard for the popular waterways newspaper *Towpath Talk*. 'When people move aboard they are confronted with the resources it takes to keep them in the style to which they have become accustomed and exactly how much waste they produce,' says Peter. 'Every resource – coal, diesel, wood, gas, food and water – must be brought onto the boat by you, and every piece of waste you produce must be disposed of by you too. Suddenly you have a personal relationship with your means of creating heat and power.'

Everything you rely on for heat, power, hygiene and cooking will run out or break eventually, often at the most inopportune moment. Murphy's Law reigns supreme on the inland waterways. Electrical systems will fail, leaving you without power unless you can fix them or pay someone else to do so. Your toilet tank will be full when you badly need to go or when you have guests arriving. It may even break down completely. Everything on a boat takes time to fix and usually costs more than you expect. The simple and idyllic boat life that you aspire to must be earned. Those who are well suited to it will not only be prepared for these eventualities, they will also have a smooth system in place for dealing with them, a backup plan for when things go wrong, and be resigned to the fact that they probably one day will. Welcome to boat life. It can sometimes be tough, but perhaps the following pages will help things run at least a little more smoothly.

Water

There is not much science involved in the provision of water on a boat. Somewhere aboard you must have a tank which, when empty, must be refilled. Ideally the tank will be situated centrally so that the constant filling and emptying does not cause your boat to list.

Steel tanks will invariably rust and need coating with specialist bitumen-based paint every few years. As a result, these steel tanks always feature a large inspection hatch for access as you will need to get inside to treat the rust and paint the interior. Plastic water tanks are often translucent, which allows you to view the water level easily, but there may not be enough visibility to allow you to inspect the contents in detail, and so some kind of removable inspection hatch is highly recommended.

Even the mains-fed water that you use to fill your tank will contain small particles of dirt, dust and other debris, and in a vessel as large as a water tank these can settle to form a layer on the bottom of the tank. Over a period this layer can

Newly painted water tanks

Remember to allow a newly painted tank to dry fully before filling and emptying the tank a couple of times prior to its first proper use. This should remove any residual paint aftertaste from the water.

Tony's Towpath Tales

Clean water?
My boat originally had two water tanks. The largest was the entire front tip of the boat and was accessible via a large hatch. The other was a small plastic tank situated below the cratch deck which was filled via a small hose hole deck fitting and fed only the cold tap in the galley. We assume that a previous owner didn't like the look of the water in the cobweb-infested rusty steel tanks and so installed a hygienic plastic one specifically to supply drinking water.

One day, shortly after buying the boat, I discovered that the plumbing to the small tank leaked, and so, after clearing up the water, I decided to remove the smaller tank completely. This was easy enough, but on inspection the small plastic tank was lined with a thick layer of disgusting green slime. I expect this was due to the boat being left unused for a long period of time, allowing the cultivation of the slime. As a result I am always wary of boats with water tanks that cannot be easily inspected. At least I can easily see the rust and the cobwebs in my large steel water tank!

become significant enough to be visible when you run the tap, causing brown or murky water to run as the tank is approaching empty. If your tank has easy access, this problem can be solved by using a pump to suck out the bottom few inches of water, running the suction hose or pipe along the bottom of your tank to suck out the debris settled there. In steel tanks it makes sense to strip and clean the tank at regular enough intervals to negate the problem, probably coinciding with the timing of a new interior coat of water tank paint. It may be advisable to use water-purifying tablets in your water tank, but these often impart an unpleasant taste themselves and seemingly few boaters use them. More often than not, those who are concerned with water purity are leisure boaters who use their water tanks infrequently and so worry about bacteria build-up. Often they use either bottled water or fill containers from their tap at home and transport them to use aboard their boat during their stay. Again, few liveaboard boaters have the patience for this and perhaps they develop a stronger immune system as a result.

Electricity

Boats with a permanent mooring have most of the convenience of a land-based home as far as electricity supply is concerned. Marinas and boatyard and boat club moorings usually have a metered electricity point for each boat, with the only break in supply being those with a token-fed meter.

An on-board charger is standard on most boats and your batteries are kept topped up for as long as you are hooked up to the mains. Conventional battery maintenance dictates that a regular discharge and recharge cycle is the best way to preserve the life and integrity of your batteries, although very few boaters adhere to this principle in practice, leaving batteries hooked up to the mains supply on constant charge.

The real test of your electrical system will happen when you are away from your mains supply and rely on your engine and alternator to charge your batteries. This is usually the time that a fault in your system becomes evident, or you finally pay the price for having your batteries on constant charge. Once the life of a full charge drops to an intolerably short number of hours you know it is time to get a new bank of batteries. It is tempting to think that installing extra batteries is a good idea and that five batteries can give you longer life between charges, but this is not the case. A few hours of engine running can only fully charge two or three leisure batteries. To charge five or more would take most of the day and constitutes a false economy. Some liveaboards use a generator to keep leisure batteries topped up, as opposed to running their boat engine. This is sometimes a cheaper option and usually more reliable than an old diesel engine during the wintertime. On the downside, generators are noisy contraptions to a greater or lesser degree and therefore

Frugal fridge-free winter

During the cold months you can switch off your fridge and keep food in your cratch area. This is most practical for those with a canvas cratch cover in order to hide their food from scavengers, but those without a cover might just use a box with a sealable lid. Be careful when telling non-boating visitors where to put the butter when they have finished with it.

Well-equipped

often found running outside the boat on the towpath to spare the boater's ears. Beware, though, that any generator on view can become a target for thieves, who can be guaranteed a booty if they wait until you leave your boat unattended. The additional risk of having petrol on board must also be seriously considered.

Most boats have a 12v electrical system installed, with appliances such as water pumps, lights and even some fridges running directly from this 12v supply. However, most modern battery-dependent appliances such as laptops, mobile phones, MP3 players and the like use a 240v supply to charge their batteries. This is not a problem when moored at a venue with mains electricity supplied, as the 240v three-pin sockets aboard will be fed directly. The issue arises when your boat is away from its mooring and mains supply, but there are a couple of ways to deal with this issue. The most common is to install an inverter which converts 12v supply to 240v, thereby bringing the three-pin sockets back into action. The downside here is that the inverter itself uses power to do its job and so essentially 'wastes' more of your batteries' power.

A more efficient solution is to use a 12v transformer, charger or adapter for the appliance you wish to use. 12v chargers are available for all mobile phones, and most laptops can be powered by a 12v transformer which can be bought separately. Travel irons and hairdryers run directly from 12v, as do mini dustbuster-type vacuum cleaners. Using a car stereo instead of a hi-fi or portable stereo system is standard on most boats, and there are even 12v TV and DVD players available too.

Walk-on solar panels

A major stumbling block for most liveaboards is the compromise that must be made regarding white goods such as refrigerators, freezers, washing machines and tumble dryers. All of these appliances can be found installed aboard boats, however, and even dishwashers are occasionally seen, but the compromises of power usage, water usage and space are significant factors to consider. For those moored permanently, power and water are less of a factor, the only inconvenience being a more regular water tank top-up. But all take up space and most are impractical or impossible to use when cruising. Refrigerators are an exception to this rule, and if you have the right fridge, most boats can enjoy refrigeration while cruising. The best choice for the liveaboard boater with cruising aspirations is one of the purpose-built 240v, 12v or gas-powered fridges. Given the running costs and convenience, gas is usually the best option to use when running a fridge. Unfortunately there is neither a gas-powered freezer, dryer, dishwasher or washing machine available ... yet!

It is important that your starter battery is somehow kept charged and separate from your leisure batteries. (If you run down your starter battery you won't be able to start your engine to recharge your leisures.) The simplest solution is to fit what is known as a split-charge relay device. This ensures that once the starter battery is fully charged it is isolated from the leisures to ensure it is available for starting the engine, even if the leisures are run flat. There are apparently many varieties of more efficient and intelligent battery management systems available, and if you understand 'electrickery', these might be worth investigating. However, many boaters stick by the philosophy that simplicity rules supreme, and many unreliable battery management systems are removed and replaced with a split-charge relay

Propane gas is used for cooking, heating and even refrigeration

Make sure you always have a spare

system. This seems to be a most common adaptation made to boats intended for liveaboard purposes, not least because the cost of maintaining and replacing management systems can be high.

Solar and wind energy can be harnessed to supplement your energy usage, and although neither is yet sufficient to exclusively power your boat, this looks set to change as renewable-energy technology advances onwards. The ability to move your boat to a sunnier spot is an advantage for those with solar panels, but be wary of theft if you are out and about on the waterways. Solar panels on the roof are a trip hazard and also take up valuable space, but this can be negated by installing 'walk-on' solar panels. These do exactly what you would expect and are a good idea if you are happy to pay the premium price they command. Wind turbines can also be installed on a boat, but some liveaboards are deterred by the constant background hum these turbines produce, although most of those who actually own one say that they soon became accustomed to it.

Gas

Propane gas in canisters is used for cooking by the vast majority of liveaboards and many use gas to produce hot water too. The size of the canister you buy will be dictated by the size of your gas locker, and most boats have lockers to accommodate 13kg bottles. Some boats do have smaller lockers, but for liveaboard purposes the smaller bottles are inconveniently small and unnecessarily expensive by unit price.

Solar junkies

Mini solar panels are put to many uses by liveaboards. Some hook them up to their starter battery to provide a constant top-up drip feed, while others use more advanced solar appliances to top up their mobile phone, MP3 player and even their laptop. Given the eco-friendly tendencies of boat folk, it seems likely that solar power will become standard installation for liveaboard boaters.

Tony's Towpath Tales

In my opinion, an Ecofan should be standard equipment on every boat with a stove. These interesting contraptions sit atop your stove and the heat makes the blades of the fan turn, thus wafting warm air to the nether regions of your boat. Costing from around £100 each (and more for the larger units), I was initially reluctant to purchase one and was dubious of their efficacy. Instead I borrowed one from a friend for a few days before he demanded it back, but by then I was totally convinced. I have since loaned mine to several unconvinced new boaters. Be careful not to drop your Ecofan as they are prone to develop an annoying rattle as the fans rotate. A refurbishment service is just about cheap enough to deter buying a new one instead, but I still prefer to stash the thing safely when setting off on a cruise.

Heat

The most common question to be asked by non-boaters is 'Is it cold in the winter?, to which my standard answer is, 'No, as long as you never let your fire go out!'

The vast majority of boats feature a multi-fuel stove to provide heat, and most use coal-type fuels of some variety. Once again, storage is the main problem with coal usage, particularly for continuous cruisers, but many marinas also apply a limit to the amount of coal you can pile up next to your boat for reasons of safety and aesthetics. Kindling is often easy to acquire cheaply or for free, but be considerate when collecting dead wood from the canalside as this has ecological consequences

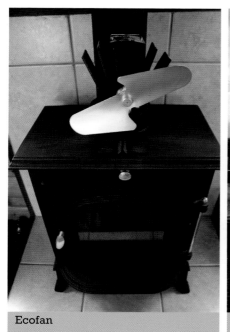

Ecofan

Liveaboards often utilise solar and wind power

Condensation

Warm air that manages to find cold steel creates condensation, and all but the most perfectly insulated boats will endure occasional drips.

(see Art of Boating chapter). There is an art to maintaining a constant and tolerable temperature within a boat and it will likely take a few months before you can manage this consistently. There is a knack to managing your stove and no two stoves are alike. It will take a few months for you to get the hang of lighting it, maintaining an even temperature and, most crucially, keeping the fire going overnight. Practice makes perfect, but it would be more realistic to accept the relationship with your stove as a truce rather than aspiring to master it completely.

Keeping the boat warm is simple compared with keeping the boat cool. During wintertime it is easy to take your eye off the ball and allow the stove to get so hot that the cabin is unbearable. During summer a steel narrowboat gets too hot to touch, and little can be done to cool it down. Having a light-coloured boat can help

Is it cold in winter?

to deflect some of the heat, but the small amount of benefit hardly outweighs the extra cleaning a light boat demands.

Stove maintenance

Maintaining multi-fuel stoves is something most boaters can do as there is not much that can go wrong, but when things do go wrong it can sometimes be expensive to rectify. Areas of likely damage include:

- **Broken glass** Cheaply and easily replaced as long as the screws holding the glass retainer in place do not shear off as you attempt to remove them.
- **Riddler** A seized or warped riddler is usually the consequence of using unsuitable fuel and running the stove at too high a temperature. Most of the coals available for boaters are suitable and can be easily managed, but the products available from petrol stations are usually 'petro-coal', which burns too hot and damages the riddler and other stove components. The convenience of a bag of petrol station coal to tide you over seems worth the extra expense until you realise the damage it causes to your stove. A new riddler will solve the problem if the grate is not warped too, otherwise replacing both is necessary.
- **Firebricks** These sometimes break, particularly in fires that have been running too hot or when bashed about during spring cleaning maintenance. These are not very expensive, but make sure you get the right product for your model of stove. There are countless different types of stove and so it is usually best to ring

Keep your stove lit and stay cosy

A boater's best friend

Happy feet

The bottom of your boat is underwater and as a result it can be terribly cold, even when the rest of the boat is warm. Thick carpets and good slippers are the only answer. A footstool or similar will be useful too, particularly if you intend to sit at a desk or table for long periods. Underfloor heating for boats is not unheard of but flies in the face of the frugal and simplistic lifestyle that is inherent with boating, and the prospect of breakdown and repair problems should discourage most boaters.

ahead to ensure the store has the ones you need in stock before setting off.

- **Flue collar** Water drips, trickles and stains are all the result of a leaky flue. Removing and resealing the collar attachment between the roof and the flue is the only solution. Look out for rust holes too, remembering to check around the back of your flue pipe. Carbon monoxide poisoning is a very real risk.
- **Stove door rope seal** These are cheap and easy to replace. Take a sample of the rope from your stove to ensure you purchase the correct thickness.
- **Flue/stove union** The seal between the stove and the flue can perish quite

Ask the Narrowboaters

Q – How do you keep your boat utilities running smoothly?

Steve and Eileen – *Rahab*

Reduce the amount of gas you buy by switching off the pilot light when you are not using the boiler. The saving is quite remarkable and cuts down the number of times you need to change the bottle significantly. The only slight inconvenience is the need to reignite the boiler each time you need hot water, but we think that is a small price to pay.

Justine and Woody – *Frog With A Heart*

As a qualified plumbing and heating engineer I really went to town designing our heating and water system. As continual cruisers we got the bulk of our electricity and hot water from running the engine. The batteries were topped up by solar panels and we had a stove with a back boiler servicing radiators and hot water during the winter. The whole system was gravity fed, so there was no need for a pump, which would have been a waste of power in my opinion. We also had a stove, simply because we like them. Nothing else gives off that kind of heat.

rapidly as the cement seal crumbles away. Be sure to check and reseal the union regularly. Along with cement, some boaters use stove door rope and copious amounts of glue to make a seal around the flue.

Diesel heaters

If you like the idea of easily controllable central heating then you might be tempted by a diesel-fuelled heater. If you go for a drip-feed diesel stove then you'll probably be pleased with these reliable and controllable heaters providing they are maintained and cleaned regularly. Be warned, though, that cleaning diesel stoves is a dirty job.

If you're thinking of a forced-air burner-style heater you might want to do some research first. Many boats have these units fitted, but stories about poor reliability are rife. It appears there is an issue with using 'red diesel' to power these units, and one manufacturer recently lost their court case, resulting in their heaters being declared 'not fit for purpose' on narrowboats. Servicing and reconditioning these units can cost around £200, with liveaboard regular usage making this expense all the more frequent. That said, there are plenty of satisfied customers using these heaters without complaint, but these appear to be the exception rather than the rule.

Hot water

Hot-water needs for leisure boaters are easily provided by using a calorifier set-up, as this system uses the engine to heat a tank of water. This is very efficient while cruising as hot water is provided for free – essentially a bonus side effect of your cruise. Even when moored it is not too inconvenient to occasionally run your engine to get enough water for showers and to boil a kettle for washing dishes and the like. Although this can become a chore for some liveaboards, others are happy with this type of set-up.

One of the most convenient arrangements is to have a gas-fuelled boiler to provide an almost instant supply of constantly hot water. This type of boiler has many benefits for the liveaboard compared to a calorifier set-up, which can only supply one tank of hot water before needing another hour or two of engine running to replenish it. The costs are difficult to compare as applications differ. For those who cruise regularly enough the calorifier system can be said to provide free hot water,

John – *Sound of Silence*
Water tanks can get a little yucky if they are left unused for any period of time. Water tank purifying tablets are available, but they leave a slight after-taste. This can be almost eliminated by installing an in-line filter to your cold water line, and it will filter our any small particles that might be in there too

Tony – *The Watchman*
Don't forget to boil your kettle on the top of your stove during winter - Free hot water!"

but in reality very few boaters cruise every day, or even every week. While using a gas-powered boiler does mean using more gas, this costs far less than the equivalent cost of running the engine for two hours while moored, simply to get hot water.

Some boats use a back boiler attached to their stove to generate free hot water. While these work well during the wintertime when the stove is lit, it is not practical to light the fire during the summer months, and so an alternative option, such as running the engine to heat a calorifier, must be installed alongside. Having two hot-water systems might seem like overkill to some, but others just can't resist the lure of occasional free hot water.

SAFE AND SOUND

Boating is no more hazardous than living in a house. Each has its own inherent risks which, with a little care, can be reduced to a negligible minimum. As with every part of our lives, knowing the risks and taking sensible precautions are the keys to staying safe. This chapter looks at the dangers and their consequences specific to the liveaboard boating lifestyle, while aiming to equip the reader with the necessary information to negate them and so reassure, rather than discourage.

Fire

The most likely and frequently observed fire risks aboard boats are multi-fuel stoves and gas-supplied appliances. Common sense and vigilance are the best protection against on-board fires, but it is worth acknowledging the boating-specific problem that such a confined space can cause. The proximity of flammable materials condensed into a liveaboard existence serves only to enhance the risk, and so extra care and close attention are recommended. Consider, too, the fact that boats can rock as you step aboard, sway in the wind and be bumped by other boats, causing otherwise safely stowed items to move or fall. It is recommended that neither stove nor cooker is lit when cruising, and these should be secured to the floor in case of a bump with another boat, bridge or lock. Most cold-weather boaters keep their stoves lit while cruising, ignoring the guidance about lit fires, so if you are one of these be sure to take special care.

Increased risk

The universal and obvious risks posed by candles and cigarettes are at least as prevalent with boaters, and some might say even more so.

An on-board gas supply is no more hazardous on a boat than it is in a home, but given that many boaters have a propensity for DIY it is important to be extra careful. When working around gas pipes or appliances the usual common sense precautions apply and a qualified person is usually necessary when working specifically on a gas appliance. Remember that propane gas is heavier than air and therefore may not be noticeable to your sense of smell at head height. Most gas alarms sold for use in houses have instructions stipulating that they should be installed in a high position, as domestic gas is lighter than air; in the case of propane gas used on boats however, these alarms should be installed near the floor.

Carbon monoxide

Again, both multi-fuel stoves and gas appliances present risks here. A carbon monoxide detector with an alarm should be a standard feature in every boat and there is no sensible reason not to. The alarm aspect of the detector is important as it is vital to be made aware of the hazard in order to take necessary action to avoid disaster. Installing a detector is not the only precaution, though. A proactive approach to prevention is advisable too: annual checking of gas appliances and a regular inspection of your stove and flue should be noted in your diary and observed religiously. Be sure to keep vents such as roof mushrooms and door vents clear. Sure, they may cause a draught during the winter, but blocking them when you are dependent on the frequent use of appliances with a carbon monoxide risk is foolishness. Remember, carbon monoxide has no smell and no taste and it cannot be seen. Vigilance is the only answer.

Sinking

The risk of sinking due to a hole in your steel hull is a small one. Having canvassed many experienced boaters, they recount very few incidents of battleship-style hull breaches. Sinking is more likely to be due to a boating incident in a lock or on a river where water is somehow allowed into the boat. Hanging the boat on a lock cill, trapping fenders and bow buttons or opening gate paddles too early are the main

Carbon monoxide checklist

- Check your stove and flue for holes caused by rust and damage.
- Check the door seal and replace the rope if necessary.
- Check the corners of your stove for holes caused by overheating expansion.
- Check the union between the stove and the flue, and also at the roof.
- Clean inside the chimney and flue at least annually, preferably more often.
- Check the flue is not blocked by ash collecting on the baffle plate inside your stove.
- Check that no on-board vents are blocked.

For more info see www.carbonmonoxidekills.com

Tony's Towpath Tales

I woke up with a headache again, for the third day in a row. I didn't worry about it too much and put it down to the fact that I rarely drink enough water and so was probably dehydrated. Besides, the headache had usually gone by the time I got to work, so I took an aspirin and drank some water and carried on with my day. First job was to check my emails.

A few days before, I had posted a question on a boating website about my stove. It had recently been acting up, not getting hot enough despite a generous loading of coal and wood. It was also belching out smoke each time I opened the door and my boat seemed to be continually full of smoke and everything smelled like Bonfire Night. One of the girls at work even thought something was on fire in the office before we realised that the smell of smoke and burning was coming from me.

At my desk with a cup of coffee I clicked on the boating website page and found my question had a few replies. I paraphrase here, but basically the replies went something like this:

'Your flue is blocked and needs cleaning.'
'If you don't do it you will die of carbon monoxide poisoning.'
'You are going to die if you don't clean your chimney.

That's "die" you understand.
Dead.'

I got the message.
   I took the morning off work and set about fixing the problem. A layer of soot, rust and ash had settled on top of the baffle plate and was blocking the flue so that air could not get in and smoke could not escape. Three hard and dirty hours later I had a clean chimney, ash an inch thick on every surface in my boat and coal ground deep into my hands. Then I spent another couple of hours doing the same job on my friend's boat. I was exhausted and black to my elbows, but at least we weren't going to die

Gongoozlers

A 'gongoozler' is someone who enjoys watching boats and boating activity. Most gongoozlers are passive observers and essentially harmless, but others will interact with boaters, usually to detrimental effect. Abusive gongoozlers are easily ignored, but those that attempt to help out or otherwise get involved can often be dangerous. Some gongoozlers even carry lock keys and windlasses and will take it upon themselves to assist with locks and bridges uninvited. Clearly there is a significant risk of sinking or damage from this type of 'help', and great care must be exercised by the boater to negate the hazard. A useful tip is to announce that you 'have a system' and that you thank them for their kind offer of help, but your process is so ingrained and habitual that it is difficult to deviate from it.

Clean-water sinking

Ruptured water tanks are unlikely to hold enough water to sink a boat, but keep a careful eye when refilling tanks from the mains to be sure the tank is holding. Add enough water to a boat with a leaking water tank and it can go down.

Barry Whitelock MBE

offenders, but the list of possible causes is long. Barry Whitelock MBE is renowned and vastly experienced, having been the resident lock-keeper of the famous Five Rise staircase locks on the Leeds-Liverpool Canal for over 20 years. 'Take your time with locks. There's no rush,' says Barry. 'Have a signal that everyone understands to alert for any problems. If there is a lock-keeper in service there then follow their advice exactly and wait for their instruction. It is their job to get you through the lock safely and efficiently.'

Mooring is another risky activity where sinking is a risk. Mooring too tightly on a waterway with variable water levels can create problems, causing your boat to tip as it rises or falls with the water. Allowing a hull skin fitting (such as an exhaust or vent) to fall below the waterline can easily cause the unthinkable to happen.

Slips and trips

Slips and trips are the most frequent and likely accidents for boaters, and particularly for liveaboards. Friction is your friend on a boat and extreme care should be taken if friction is compromised. Boats and pontoons are equally hazardous and it is easy to be careless. Water is the most usual culprit, particularly if it is frozen as snow or ice, but diesel and oil spills are common slip hazards too. Always step onto a wet surface squarely as it is surprising how fast your foot can slide sideways from under you. Bumps, breaks and bruises are painful, but usually easily fixed. It is the risk of head injury and drowning that is the main concern, particularly if you are alone when it happens as most liveaboards generally are.

Gongoozlers

Good windlass technique

Anti-slip safety tips

- Many liveaboards have a whistle attached to their boat keys in the hope that if they were to slip and need help, the whistle would be available to attract attention.

- Locks and bridges are particularly hazardous and it goes without saying that extreme care should be exercised.

- Spilled diesel and oil are severe slip hazards and should be cleaned up immediately.

- Never jump onto or off a boat. Step aboard or ashore comfortably, and if this is not possible, move the boat closer.

- Never jump onto the roof of a boat from a lock or from another boat.

- Highlight mooring pins with hi-vis material or white plastic bags.

- Keep ropes coiled and out of the way and the roof free of trip hazards, particularly when cruising.

- Clean the roof regularly as leaves, mud, soot and slime will increase the risk of slips.

- Step squarely onto wet boats and pontoons as sideways momentum can cause your foot to slip from under you in wet or slippery conditions.

Rooftop equipment can be a trip hazard

Keep ropes coiled and tidy

- Never get blasé about the risk of slips and falls on a boat. Falling onto a steel boat can break bones and cause head injuries, and the risk of falling into the water while unconscious is a very real one.

A key float is a useful precaution.
Photo by Jo Bowling

Vandalism and break-ins

Even in the most salubrious of neighbourhoods, it is impossible to eradicate the risk of vandalism or burglary completely and so it is wise to take sensible precautions to deter the perpetrators. The most obvious method is to select your mooring places carefully. It is often worth speaking with local boaters and lock-keepers and be prepared to avoid notorious trouble hot spots. Town centres often suffer the usual antisocial problems caused by late-night revellers. Noise, litter and peeing in your plant pots are unpleasant sufferances to bear, but actual vandalism is thankfully uncommon.

Porthole power

Portholes are more secure against break-in than the larger types of window, which are usually very easy to remove. Louvre windows are particularly vulnerable to break-in.

Ask the Narrowboaters

Q – What is your top safety tip?

Steve and Eileen – *Rahab*
Unless your dog is perfectly behaved, do not allow them on deck when you are cruising. We have seen dogs launch themselves off boats to try to get at another on the towpath, we have seen them trip people up as they are stepping ashore, and we even once saw a dog fall overboard while tied to the boat by its lead.

Darren – *Dunster*
If I am cruising or working on the boat I always empty my pockets of vulnerable valuables, just in case I fall in. Similarly, I never hold my keys in my hand as I step on or off the boat as I'd hate to slip and fling them into the water. At least if they are in my pocket when I fall in I will still have them when I get out.

Burglar alarms for boats are available but few boaters find them necessary. Some of these alarms have motion sensors which emit an electronic beep as you near the boat – highly irritating for those moored nearby. Canvas covers at the bow or stern provide nominal protection for items stored within, but also provide cover for intruders to work unseen on your security. Good padlocks seem to deter all but the most determined burglar, but it must be accepted that it is easy to get into any boat if the intruder is determined enough. Given that there is little space or inclination to collect high value possessions, most boaters are more fearful of vandalism than of burglary, but remember neither experience is common on the waterways.

Boaters occasionally experience antisocial behaviour while cruising or when stopped to use locks or bridges, often from youths or children. Good interpersonal skills will usually deter bad behaviour, and briefly engaging with the local youth can stop problems before they start. If bad behaviour does occur, the best advice is to use your mobile phone, firstly to call the police and then to photograph or record the perpetrators. This usually brings an end to the episode very swiftly.

Dog lifejacket

Choose your mooring spots wisely

Illness and disease

Canal water is home to some rather unsavoury stuff. While much of it will result only in mild stomach upsets, Weil's disease (also known as leptospirosis) is potentially fatal. Incidents of Weil's disease are rare and deaths from it are rarer still, but as with all risks, it is worth knowing how to avoid it and what to do if you suspect you may have contracted it.

Weil's disease is transmitted through contact with animal urine which, most notably for canal users, will usually be from rats. It is found in stagnant, still or slow-moving water and also on canal and river banks. It is contracted through contact with the mouth, eyes, ears, nose or open wounds on the body. Falling into the water, handling wet ropes and even wet or muddy shoes can potentially pose a risk.

Cleanliness is the best precaution, washing hands thoroughly before eating

Woody – *Frog With A Heart*
As one qualified to work with LPG boating gas I have come across some truly shocking DIY gas installations. They are not common, but for the sake of safety it makes sense to get your gas system inspected by someone who knows what they are looking for, and has the right equipment to find and fix any faults that might exist.

John – *Sound of Silence*
If someone falls overboard, cut the engine immediately. Once in the water most people are compelled to swim back towards the stern because this is the lowest part of the boat. Unfortunately that is where the propeller is.

Weil's disease symptoms

- Headaches
- Fever
- Chills
- Malaise
- Vomiting
- Muscle pain, particularly in the calf muscles
- Bruising and bleeding beneath the skin

and drinking and taking care to avoid other contaminations via the mouth. All contact with the water should be considered a risk and so procedures such as working in the weed hatch could cause a problem, particularly if you have scratches or other open wounds on your hands and arms. Boat life being what it is, open wounds and scratches are a regular occurrence, so understanding the risks is important. Be careful, too, when clearing debris from around your prop through the weed hatch, as fishing twine and hooks are commonly found there.

Of course, should you fall into the water the possibility of contracting Weil's increases. It is recommended that you shower immediately and see a doctor as soon as possible as a precautionary measure, explaining what has happened and your concern about Weil's.

Knowing the symptoms of Weil's is important if you contract the disease unwittingly. Most of the symptoms are akin to those you get when you have a cold or flu, and the odds are that if you have these symptoms you probably do have just that. But be aware and be prepared to act accordingly if you experience these symptoms, and be sure to stress your concerns about Weil's disease to your doctor.

Canal towpaths and riversides are popular venues for dog walkers too. Unfortunately, some dog owners are not as conscientious as they should be and dog poo is a frequent waterside hazard. Inadvertently walking dog poo into the boat and grabbing ropes that have been similarly fouled is enormously exasperating. Boaters with first-hand experience of this will understand the restraint that has been exercised when writing this section, as the desire to use more industrial language is overwhelming.

Contamination

Sealing your water tank against contamination is a wise precaution.

Drinking and boating

Relaxation is often accompanied by a glass of wine or a cold beer, and so it would appear that boating and drinking could be lots of fun. Unlike when driving a car, there is no law against boating and drinking, but rest assured that if an accident were to occur as a result of intoxication it is likely that someone would be found to be at fault and made liable. Very careful alcohol consumption is recommended while aboard.

Tony's Towpath Tales

I was once moored up at a boatyard abreast a boat with a cruiser stern. In order to get onto my boat from the bank I had to walk across the cruiser deck, which was fine during the light of day, but one evening as I left my boat in the dark I did not notice that someone had removed the deck boards to work on the engine. Stepping off my boat I fell into the engine bay of the cruiser, ending up at the bottom in a crumpled mess and in terrible pain. Thankfully it was nothing that a few stitches could not put right, but from that day on I never leave my boat without my head torch if it is dark. Few mooring places have adequate lighting and boat life seems to be littered with trip hazards, so I cite a head torch as the most useful piece of boating equipment.

10

THAT'S ENTERTAINMENT

It is easy to see why many liveaboard boaters forego the use of electronic entertainment devices: having downsized to a more simplistic existence, the joys of activities such as reading, walking, cycling and board games seem to fit the lifestyle more comfortably. There is no need to exclude modern technology from liveaboard life entirely, however, particularly when moored at a venue with mains electricity supply. Even when cruising, most appliances can be used aboard a boat if the owner desires it enough. Finding a balance between the power requirements of the appliance and the cost and inconvenience of running the boat's engine to recharge batteries will determine your usage.

Computers and the internet

Few boaters use conventional tower-style computers, preferring laptop units for versatility and space-saving purposes. Powering an average laptop through an inverter from a boat with two leisure batteries will result in around four or five hours of continual usage, so 12v chargers are useful for boaters who use their laptop extensively. Smaller notebook-size appliances will be more than adequate for most boaters as these can last for much longer periods on one charge of their battery. External hard drives are useful for storing music, films and photographs and negate the need for a larger, more power-hungry computer.

Only bona fide residential moorings will feature a phone line capable of providing broadband Internet access, but this is not a problem for the modern liveaboard boater as there are many alternative means to surf the Net. Today the Internet is so easily accessed from a wide variety of appliances that some boaters dispense with the need for a computer completely. Smartphones and tablets can allow access to the internet with functionality enough for emailing and occasional web browsing. However, laptops remain the most popular on-board means of using the Internet and connection speeds have improved vastly since the early days of remote connection. Using a 3G dongle is almost as fast as a home broadband service and connection can cost as little as £10 per month (at time of print) on a contract or by pay as you go. The system uses mobile phone-style SIM cards and signals and therefore dongles are available from all mobile phone suppliers.

Tethering

It is possible to access the Internet for free by linking up a laptop via a smartphone. Known as 'tethering', it is frowned upon by some service providers and some may cap the amount of data available to users via the smartphone for this reason. Others might charge a premium. It is not easy to set up for those of us without the requisite credentials, and even then, the service is comparatively slow. All of these problems are likely to be resolved soon, but until then, for those who can be bothered and have the right contract, Internet access could be free.

Some marinas offer wireless Internet connection, either for free or with a small monthly charge. The reliability of the service is often dependent on proximity to the host router, but the service is rarely tied to a contract. Signal boosters are available to optimise the connection, but frugal boaters will research how to make one themselves in true *Blue Peter* style. Of course, if your signal is really bad you might not be able to log on to the Internet to do the research in the first place.

Sometimes it is possible to 'piggyback' an unsecured wireless network, particularly in built-up residential areas, but the jury is out as regards the legality of this type of free surfing. Some consider it theft, as you are consuming a commodity that someone else is paying for, although few home broadband connections have metered access or download limits nowadays. Others make the analogy that although we did not pay for the flowers we can see and smell in someone's garden, we can still enjoy the benefits without anyone incurring a cost as a result. Your call …

Surf the web with a laptop and a dongle

Playing CDs uses a surprising amout of power

Mobile Wi-Fi Internet

As this book was being completed, a new mobile wireless service became available that allows more than one person to access the Internet from anywhere on the boat. It works through a small device which sends and receives data like a 3G dongle, but then transmits a wireless connection to whichever users log in. Currently the prices for data are comparable to and sometimes better than those available for dongle users. Early reviews state that the service is usually reliable, quicker and certainly more convenient than using a dongle.

Television and film

Freeview and Freesat services are available, with signal being remarkably good in most parts of the network. Boat-friendly aerials are available at many chandleries and there is even a portable device on the market. With TVs being a relatively large drain on battery power, many liveaboards do not own one, although this is often related to the desire to 'unsubscribe' from modern lifestyles and conventional culture. Watching movies using a laptop or portable DVD player is one possible compromise, but be wary of downloading films from the Internet via your dongle as this amount of data will swallow your allowance in no time.

Smartphones to the rescue – again

Instead of owning a separate MP3 player you might consider loading your music collection onto your smartphone and linking it to an on-board car stereo via cable or FM radio transmitter. Not only does this negate the need to buy a separate MP3 player, it also means you have less to lose if your boat is broken into, as your appliance and music collection have probably been taken ashore with you.

Ask the Narrowboaters

Q – What's your main source of entertainment?

Darren – *Dunster*
My guitar.

Debbie – *Dunster*
Darren's guitar or my iPod.

Tony – *The Watchman*
My laptop for Internet access, audiobooks, films and music.

John – *Sound of Silence*
I read lots of books and occasionally watch TV.

Steve and Eileen – *Rahab*
Board games, wildlife spotting and amateur meteorology.

Music

Mains-operated music systems are usually ignored in favour of 12v car stereos. In addition to the power-efficient usage of the 12v supply, these have the added advantage of being resistant to the vibrations of boat engines. The transition from CDs to MP3 format has not made too many ripples as most car stereos can easily be wired to an MP3 player. Alternatively, you might use an ingenious gadget, an FM radio transmitter, that attaches to your MP3 player and sends your chosen music to your car stereo via an FM radio signal. This allows you to store all of your music in one place and control your playlist regardless of where you are in your boat. Laptops wired up to speaker systems are an option but getting good sound quality can be expensive. Wind-up and solar-powered radios are very efficient and therefore ideal for liveaboard boaters needing to minimise drain on their boat's battery bank.

Tony's Towpath Tales

Running my laptop and charging my mobile phone are probably the biggest drains on my battery power reserves. I'm at my desk for up to ten hours a day and my laptop is switched on at 8am and doesn't get turned off until I fall asleep at night. Most of that time during the day I am working, but it also gets used to play DVDs in the evening and I always fall asleep to an audiobook.

This extensive use of my laptop isn't a problem while I am moored with shore power, but being out and about is a monumental pain in the backside. The battery life of every laptop I have ever owned has been next to useless, so I am mostly reliant on charging it with my inverter, which means running the engine to recharge the batteries for a couple of hours every day. This year I intend to address the issue once and for all. I intend to purchase a 12v charger and get a 12v socket installed near my desk, and as soon as this laptop dies my next machine will be a notebook with better power efficiency. But my main means of assault on the power problem is going to be solar powered in the form of walk-on solar panels, which should keep my batteries topped up for most of the time, at least until running the engine will not interfere with my fragile concentration.

Games consoles

Although most boaters might baulk at the idea of a games console on board, some do have them and some would consider them a necessity. Darren lives aboard with his partner Debbie and their teenage son Jake. 'He's an outdoor boy for sure, but games consoles are as much a necessity for kids his age as a bicycle and a laptop. This is the 21st century!' All games consoles are easily accommodated if you have shore power hook-up, but small portable devices such as the PSP are a better choice when you are reliant on battery power only. Darren continues, 'We cruised for seven hours one day while the boy wonder was inside using a PlayStation via the inverter. When we reached our destination it wasn't long before our leisure batteries were flat. The PlayStation was using power as fast as we were generating it!' Online gaming is not currently possible without a landline broadband and so is not an option for most boaters.

11

DIRTY FINGERNAILS

If you own a boat you should be prepared to get your hands dirty. Even a brand-new boat in A1 condition will require a hands-on approach to keep you afloat and fully functional. Boating is a dirty-fingernails kind of lifestyle and your boat will require constant attention. Although generic boat maintenance and management has been discussed elsewhere in this book, it is important to look at this issue from a purely liveaboard perspective.

One of the major reasons for liveaboard boaters returning to dry land is that they have been unprepared to deal with the consequences of bad boat maintenance and equipment breakdowns. Malfunctions can sometimes be costly and are always frustrating, and while they cannot be avoided completely, regular boat maintenance, a good toolbox and a 'can do' attitude are certainly required. Unlike for weekend boaters, going home and leaving it to be fixed another day is not an option.

A good rule of thumb is to never half-do a job. A quick fix should only be considered a temporary measure, as a collection of bodge jobs and workarounds will quickly make boat life unbearable. Each time something goes wrong with anything on the boat, think 'How can I fix this so it does not happen again?' Often this will mean replacing whatever is in place with a more suitable system or product, usually one that is easy to maintain and repair. Boat life seems to attract people with the requisite handy skills and so it is often possible to tackle small jobs yourself or with the help of a friendly neighbour. However, sometimes the only answer is to dig deep and hire a professional.

Electrics

'Electrical problems are by far the most frequent cause of breakdowns,' says Jo from Snaygill Boats. 'Alternator, starter motor, battery management and charging problems can close down a boat.' Most often the problem has been hidden while the boat is moored up with shore power, only becoming apparent when cruising makes the boater reliant on the battery system. Typically the problem originates from constant charging of the batteries from the shore supply. Over time this process gradually dries the batteries and makes them unable to hold a charge for any length of time. Of course, the boater only finds out that their batteries are dead when they set off on a cruise and find that they have no power. Having a battery management system in place can negate this problem, providing the system stays functional. Regardless, it is a good idea to test your battery system occasionally in the comfort of your own home mooring by unplugging from the mains for a period and using the engine to recharge your system. The discharge-then-recharge process is good for your batteries and will reassure you that everything is working as it should.

Toilets

Toilet problems come a close second in the frustration and inconvenience stakes. A full toilet tank that will not pump out is an urgent and unpleasant problem to fix. Poking around with sticks inside the tank can often solve the issue temporarily, but eventually a permanent solution will be required.

Making sure that foreign bodies that can cause a blockage are not put into your black water tank is common sense, but in addition you should ensure that the usual contents do not solidify (see chapter on toilets). Do not scrimp on toilet fluids as generous use will usually prevent the problem, but an occasional blast with a jet wash device will help too. Cassette toilet owners are advised to have a spare cassette to use should one fail or be unexpectedly full, and pump-out users are advised to have a cassette toilet in reserve in readiness for the same problems.

Fair warning

Macerator toilets will often die slowly, giving you plenty of warning that they are about to fail. Be ready to tackle the issue before it becomes a major problem.

Water

Water systems often fail during the wintertime when cold weather and thaws can cause burst pipes. Although this is more of a problem for weekend boaters who do not keep their boats warm while they are not aboard, it can affect liveaboards too. Hiding plumbing behind the fit-out joinery might be aesthetically pleasing but this makes it more susceptible to cold-weather problems. Pipes that can be kept warm while the boat is being heated will solve the issue for most liveaboards, but a vigilant watch for leaks is still advisable. Even during the summer, leaks are possible due to the increased usage a liveaboard boat system gets. Water pumps and shower drain gulpers break down frequently for this reason and it is worth having a spare on hand as a quick replacement.

Water tanks can also develop leaks and faults, most commonly being caused by collisions and bumps when boating. A poorly secured tank containing hundreds of litres of water can shift significantly in a collision, causing fixings, pipes and filler inlets to fracture.

Leaky window frames are the bane of many liveaboards, particularly those with older boats. The constant heating and cooling of the steel and woodwork and the deterioration of ageing sealant can cause formerly sound window frame seals to leak and subsequently rust. The only definitive solution is to remove the window, treat the rust and then properly replace and reseal it. However, this can ruin the look of a nice paint job, so it is easy to see why boaters might be reluctant to bite this particular bullet. A temporary fix by applying silicone or another similar sealant to the edges of the frame might stop the rot for a short while, but rest assured the problem will return eventually.

Free quick fix

If the frame leaks from the top edge, then those with hopper-style windows can open the top flap to catch the drip so that it runs outside the boat.

Weed hatch and stern gland

A common problem when cruising is for debris to collect around the boat prop, so having the right tools to remove it will speed up the job considerably. Wire-cutters, bolt croppers, pliers, mole grips, a very sharp knife and lots of colourful language will usually suffice. Listen out for rattles and keep an eye on the engine temperature and the revs-to-speed ratio.

Sinking

Each year many boats sink or narrowly avoid sinking because the lid to the weed hatch has not been adequately secured. Water from a poorly fixed weed hatch can fill an engine bay in seconds.

A stern gland is the threshold between the interior of your boat and the water outside and is packed with grease and a specialist filler rope to seal against leaks. A tap attached to a cylinder of grease is turned after each cruise to force grease into the gland to keep it packed and waterproof. However, the whole gland will deteriorate over time and will require removing and repacking occasionally, usually once every couple of years. The need for this job to be done becomes evident when your engine bay and bilges begin to collect water even after you have applied grease by turning the tap after each cruise. The bilge pump, which removes the inevitable water collecting there, will solve the job temporarily as the condition worsens, but you will soon need to tackle the problem. It is a fiddly job that requires careful execution to ensure it is done correctly, but it is well within the scope of most boaters. Those with trad boats might find access difficult.

Cleaning up a leak

A good piece of advice is to never let a drip turn into a leak, but if a leak does occur you will need some means of removing the water from your boat. Most boats have an inspection hatch in the floor somewhere near the stern of the boat. Regular checks here will reassure you that all is well with your water system, but if you discover water here then you need to find out where the problem is. Thankfully the water in the inspection hatch is usually clean water rather than canal water, indicating that the problem lies in the boat's plumbing system.

Once the problem is located and fixed, your next job is to remove the water from the bilges. A spare bilge pump that can be wired up to a battery will do the job in most cases, but if you have a lot of water there it is quicker to use a toilet pump-out system. Be aware that water will have gathered in all of the nooks and crannies of ballast under the floor of your boat and will probably take a few days to make its way to the inspection hatch before you pump it out. This is a good reason to never use gravel or sand as ballast, although it is not uncommon to find it used in old boats. Once most of the water has been removed using pumps, the easiest way to collect the last remaining mess is with disposable nappies. Nappies soak up large amounts of water in just a few minutes and are then easily removed and disposed of. Be sure not to leave them in place for more than a few hours as they quickly deteriorate and fall apart, becoming another difficult clean-up job in themselves. Another option is to use an aquavac and empty it regularly, or to scatter cat litter and use a dustpan and brush to remove it when the water has been absorbed.

Flooring

Your choice of flooring makes a huge difference to your quality of life. Each type has its pros and cons and there is no single universally accepted choice. Although it is not integral to the workings of the boat or its utilities, old or unsightly flooring can spoil your enjoyment and be expensive to replace.

Flooring	Pros	Cons
Carpet	Is warm to walk on and has insulating properties. Easily and cheaply replaced, particularly if using tiles.	Vacuum cleaners use lots of power. Needs replacing regularly as mud and other soiling is walked in off the towpath.
Wooden flooring	Very attractive.	Susceptible to damp and does not flex with boat movements making it entirely unsuitable.
Laminate flooring	Modern and attractive. Easily cleaned without a vacuum cleaner	Expensive to fit. Cold underfoot. Irritatingly noisy for dog owners.
Lino	Cheap and easy to install. Easily cleaned.	Cold underfoot. Aesthetically unpopular.

Tony's Towpath Tales

Having replaced my boat's carpets twice I decided I wanted to install flooring that does not get dirty so quickly. After discounting wood and laminate (they warp when wet) and lino (ugly), I decided a rubber floor would be the most suitable choice. Waterproof, hard-wearing, easily cleaned and insulating, it seemed just the job. I looked at several types of rubber flooring, including playground substrates and gym flooring, but all were very expensive. In the end I chose matting sold in the equestrian market for stable floors. It was much cheaper than all of the other rubber options and did everything I needed it to do. The only issue I found was that when it was first delivered and fitted it had a strong rubbery smell, but this wore off after a few weeks. I am very happy with my choice as it is attractive, waterproof, insulating, easy to clean and does not make an awful 'tippy tap' noise when my dog walks on it.

Stove leaks

The union between the stove flue and the stove collar fitting on the roof is an occasional source of leaks. Although this looks to be a complicated job it is actually quite simple, if a little time-consuming. Removing the brass dressing from around the flue inside the boat will grant access to the fibreglass packing between the flue and the collar. Remove this before going outside the boat to tackle the roof collar. Remove the bolts holding the collar in place before checking that the collar is not sealed to the flue by cement or sealant. If so, you might need to use a drill to break up and then remove the cement. You may need to employ stern persuasion in order to remove the collar as lots of sealant is generally used to install them. Once removed, clean all sealant and rust from both the collar and the roof before applying a rust treatment to the affected areas. Use a flexible heat-resistant sealant to reinstall the collar, being sure to add a bead around the interior and the exterior edges as well as around the

Chimney tips

- A double-skin chimney will stop tar from leaking into your boat from burnt wood.
- Beware that chimney coolie hats can drip this tar onto your exterior paintwork.
- Removing and storing your chimney inside your boat during the summer months will extend its life considerably.
- Secure your chimney to the boat with a thin chain so that it will not fall into the water if kicked or fouled on a low bridge.

You will need a good tool kit

securing bolt holes. Replace new fibreglass packing to fill the hole between collar and flue from inside the boat, and use stove cement to pack the remaining space between from outside. Finally, ensure that the union between the stove and the flue is secure and refurbish it if required.

Engine maintenance

Engine maintenance is important for all boaters, but liveaboards who rely on their engine to charge their batteries have an added incentive. Annual servicing is recommended, but be sure you can do the job fully and efficiently before tackling it yourself. Jo from Snaygill Boats explains why: 'We get lots of boats brought to us with problems caused by self-servicing. Either the job has been abandoned once the owner realised it was more than they could handle or we end up repairing the consequences of poor servicing attempts. Learning how to service your own boat is great if you learn how to do it properly, but a badly maintained boat is just going to cause problems at some point in the future.'

Diesel bug

Diesel bug issues are becoming more prevalent for a whole range of vehicles, not just narrowboats, and the problem is getting worse. The bug is a microbial organism that lives and breeds in the fuel tank, specifically in the interface between your fuel and any water that has contaminated it. Water gets into your tank either by accidental contamination or when condensation forms as the internal tank temperature changes. Contaminations can be seen as a black sludge that affects the fuel line, particularly the filters. The bug breeds best at temperatures of 30–40

Ask the Narrowboaters

Q – How do you cope with boat maintenance?

Steve and Eileen – *Rahab*

We tackle stuff as it becomes an issue. Neither of us is particularly keen on DIY, so we have no great compulsion to do any more than is necessary to keep things ticking along. We're not particularly precious about our boat's exterior either. Boating is a contact sport and bumps will inevitably happen. Scratches and scrapes don't make any practical difference to how the boat works. One good thing about living aboard is that housework only takes a matter of minutes!

Justine and Woody – *Frog With A Heart*

A white or light-coloured engine bay is a good idea. Not only are oil leaks easy to spot but it makes visibility a little better in this otherwise dull space.

degrees Celsius, making narrowboat fuel tanks an ideal environment, given the proximity to the engine bay and the heat produced there.

The European legislation for all diesels to have at least a 5% content of biofuel has exacerbated the problem as the organic material it contains is an ideal substrate for diesel bug. The problem may become worse still as the mandatory proportion of biofuel in the mix is likely to increase again.

Prevention of diesel bug is difficult, if not impossible. Keeping your fuel tank full, particularly during winter, will reduce the amount of condensation created within the tank, but it is thought that most diesel is contaminated to some degree in the supply chain during normal handling and storage. There are also several treatments available to combat the problem, such as chemicals and magnetised units to fit to the fuel line. One glimmer of hope is that the problem also affects the road haulage industry and therefore a reliable and cost-effective solution will probably become available to protect this enormous industry from losses.

Top DIY Tip

A spirit level is of no use whatsoever on a boat.

Liveaboard boater's tool kit

- Adjustable spanner
- Angle grinder
- Bailing device – jug or similar
- Bilge pump
- Bolt croppers
- Bow saw
- Cable ties
- Chainsaw
- Cordless drill and driver
- Disposable nappies
- Dustpan and brush
- Electrical screwdriver
- Electrical tape
- Funnels
- Gaffer tape
- Goggles and mask
- Hammer
- Hatchet or hand axe
- Head torch
- Jigsaw
- Jubilee clip
- Latex gloves
- Mole grips

- Pliers
- Ratchet screwdriver with various bits
- Selection of nuts, bolts, screws and tacks
- Silicone sealant and gun
- Socket set
- Spanners in metric and imperial sizes
- Stanley knife and replacement blades
- Tape measure
- Wire-cutters
- Wiring-locator device
- Wood saw

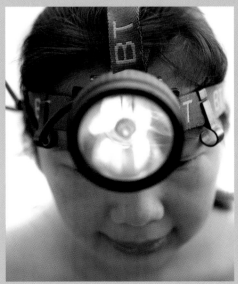

Head Torch – Essential liveaboard kit

12

EVERYDAY MATTERS

Once you introduce ambiguity to your residential status by moving aboard a boat, you often slip through the gaps in the network of modern society. Most offices of officialdom will ask for your name and address, and unless you can give an answer that is acceptable to their computer system you'll probably experience problems. Everything from your driving licence to your access to health care and financial services can be affected, and unless you want to hide from the world entirely you need to be prepared to find a solution. Submitting a tax return, registering to vote, claiming benefits and even getting an OAP bus pass is complicated for those without a recognised conventional permanent address, but there are ways to deal with the issue. Continuous cruisers are most vulnerable to the problems that living aboard can cause, and often the only answer is to rely on the safety net provided for those who are homeless.

One solution is to use an address that is accepted as your official residence, such as that of a charitable friend or member of your family. While this may seem the most simple and suitable answer, the location of that address and its proximity to your current mooring defines how effective a solution it actually is. Postal services, couriers and registering with doctors and onto the electoral roll are all problematic if your official address is nowhere near your mooring spot.

Doctors and other medical services

Of course, you can get treatment in an emergency at any local hospital with an A&E department, but you can still experience problems if you need to call an ambulance or have a doctor visit you aboard. Although it is rare, there have been occasions of both ambulance crews and GPs refusing to board a boat for health and safety reasons, despite the health of the patient being seemingly at greater risk. Even registering with a doctor can be difficult (see below), so be ready to find a way to fit into the system they have in place. NHS Direct is a very useful service, if only to determine whether you do in fact need to visit a doctor. The service is available online or by phone, and although nine times out of ten you will be told to visit your GP for treatment, it is reassuring and helpful to speak with someone who can (usually) diagnose your condition.

Tony's Towpath Tales

I'd been at my new mooring for a couple of months when I fell ill and needed to visit the doctor. On arrival at the surgery I was asked for my address which, when I told them I lived on a boat, caused something of a commotion. My official address was in another county and the address of my boat club mooring was not listed on their database, so they were not sure that they could accept me as a patient unless I could prove that I lived in the area. It was eventually suggested that unless I was intending to be in the area for a 'decent period of time' I should not register, and would need to visit my old GP instead, some 120 miles away. I explained that being a boater it was likely that I would be moving around quite a lot and so I could not guarantee that I would be in the area for 'a decent period of time' – whatever that might be. However, as I was obviously sick at that moment and they were currently my local surgery, I said I would be grateful if they could register me there and arrange for me to see a doctor. Still there appeared to be some reluctance and they were clearly not comfortable for me to register. In the end I told them that I had just decided that I would be staying in the area for the rest of my life and gave the address of my local friend! I was seen by the doctor and consoled myself that although their system didn't accommodate my circumstances I had still managed to get the treatment I needed.

Finding out your nearest A&E department is advisable when new to a mooring.
Photo: Stephen Finn/Shutterstock.com

Without a permanent address, some job applications will become tricky

Some local NHS districts offer walk-in health centre facilities akin to GP services for non-registered patients, although these are not available everywhere and your nearest centre may still be some distance away. Some large cities have similar private sector clinics but these will inevitably charge for the services and convenience they provide. Another option for minor injuries and illnesses is an NHS Walk-in Centre. These are staffed by nurses and you do not need to register or have an appointment to visit them. Their services overlap those offered by doctors and hospitals, covering infection and rashes, fractures and lacerations, emergency contraception and advice, stomach upsets, cuts and bruises and burns and strains. However, they are not set up to deal with ongoing health problems or life-threatening emergencies.

Postal and courier deliveries

Although most mooring providers do not offer residential moorings, some have provision to receive mail for those with boats moored there. The risk here is that by receiving mail at a mooring address it can be perceived as evidence that the mooring provider is breaking their planning terms by accommodating liveaboards, and so many marinas draw the line at providing this service. Some still do, though, and a little detective work can help you to spot when mail services are available at a mooring provider site.

In most places it is possible to use a 'Poste Restante' service. French for 'post remaining' this is a free service that was popular historically and is intended for those without a specific address. It enables itinerants to collect mail from a post office or sorting office near to their current location. Finding a post office or sorting office that still remembers, understands and offers this service is rather a pot luck process, and some will simply bluster or refuse to accommodate it. Usually the mail is addressed to the recipient using the address of the collection office or sorting office and marked 'POST RESTANTE', but others use the address of the recipient's mooring, knowing that the letter can go no further than the most local sorting office. In either case it is imperative to establish an understanding with the local staff at the office to ensure it all goes smoothly. Some marinas have had this system in place for many years, with boaters and office staff being on first-name terms.

Courier deliveries for those without a specific address can be even more problematic as the service is more sporadically used and relationships are more difficult to nurture. Often couriers will arrive at a postcode looking for a house with an interesting name. Unless the recipient is on constant watch for the puzzled courier the parcel will go back to the depot, and with nowhere to leave a calling card, you'll never know that they have been. Occasionally a long-serving delivery driver will keep the same patch for years and get to know the contact details for local boaters, but this is a rare occurrence and cannot be relied upon. There are a couple of solutions, the first being to request that the sender lists a mobile phone number on the address label of the package. This is a reasonably reliable workaround, but occasionally the sender manages to omit the number from the label, or the delivery driver misses the number or doesn't want to call it from his own mobile phone. A more reliable option is to have the parcel delivered to your place of work or to a local friend if these options exist. While it would not be acceptable to use such addresses for official address purposes, most employers (and friends) are happy to receive the occasional package.

Banks and other service providers

Not being able to get mail delivered to your mooring can cause significant problems when being asked for proof of your address. The requirements of banks and other service providers such as mobile phone services vary greatly. Some require proof in triplicate of a registered address that they have listed on their database, whereas others have a more flexible approach. As a general rule it can be much more problematic to set up a new account with a new organisation than it is to change an address with an existing one. This can force boaters to stick with a company not through loyalty or because they offer the best product or service, but because the prospect of changing supplier is so fraught with difficulty. Again, the easiest solution is to have one single registered land address where all formal correspondence is delivered. The problems of proximity are negated in most cases, as statements, bills and invoices can be viewed online. Internet banking is fast becoming the standard norm too, and most bills and transfers are easily done on the Net.

The matter gets complicated when companies require several different proofs of address. If you use different addresses for different services you may find that you do not have enough to give a proof of address for one specific place. Most will expect to see utilities bills, but as boaters do not use gas, electric or water supply companies these are not an option. Most companies will not recognise correspondence from British Waterways as official proof, and the lack of a landline, broadband and TV service providers narrows the field even more. Given the headaches that proof-of-address requests can cause, it is worth keeping a log of all the organisations you need to notify when you change your mooring. Keeping them up to date with your current whereabouts will ensure that you have as many options as possible when providing proof of address. Thankfully, most commercial organisations are keen enough to attract and keep customers that they are happy to go the extra mile to accommodate those with unusual circumstances, and explaining your liveaboard lifestyle to the operative taking your application will usually bring about a satisfactory result.

Benefits

It is possible to claim benefits as a liveaboard boater. Claiming housing benefit to cover mooring fees appears relatively simple and some boaters have even managed to have their licence fee awarded too. When claiming these benefits it would make sense to claim council tax benefit too, if indeed you are one of the very few boaters who actually pay it. And therein lies the problem. By claiming housing benefit and council tax your liveaboard status becomes very noticeable, official and undeniable. A mooring provider that does not have the relevant planning permission for residential moorings would understandably take exception to any official statement that they are harbouring a liveaboard, often resulting in them tightening the mooring rules. The consequences for liveaboards down on their luck and reliant upon benefits might be severe, as the likelihood of losing a mooring should not be underestimated. While there are many cases of liveaboards finding a niche in the system where claiming benefits is possible, there is inevitably an inherent stress and vulnerability that comes with the situation and extreme caution should be employed.

Tax credits are the responsibility of HMRC rather than the local council and there appears to be little communication between the two agencies.

Ask the Narrowboaters

Q – Does a lack of a permanent address make life difficult?

Justine and Woody – *Frog With A Heart*
No, not really. All of our mail was sent to a 'care of' address and picked up when we had the chance, although I did once almost miss jury service because I didn't see the letter until the day before. But for the most part it is just about being resourceful.

Darren – *Dunster*
When buying stuff from eBay or online shops I always ask that the item is posted. Using the post is always more reliable than trying to deal with couriers.

TV Licensing

There are no specific rules regarding TV licensing for liveaboard boaters, and even those who attempt to obtain one often run into problems. If you have a land address with a TV licence your viewing aboard is covered under this. If you have a residential mooring where you are permanently dwelling you will need (and can easily acquire) a TV licence specifically for that bona fide address. However, those boaters without a specific address seem to slip between the gaps of the licensing regulations.

Interestingly, TV licence inspectors have very few powers to investigate licence evasion, even when investigating those watching TV in a land-based house. Mere ownership of a TV, aerial or set-top box does not necessitate a licence; a licence is only required to receive and view a TV programme, and so unless it can be proved that someone was actually watching, enforcement of the licence regulations is very difficult indeed. Licensing officials have no right to enter property without a warrant, and ownership of TV broadcast-receiving equipment is no proof of licence evasion. All things considered, it appears that the TV licensing authorities have decided that the cost and inconvenience of enforcing the regulations within the boating community are not worth the hassle considering the small numbers involved.

Dating

Boaters often live aboard alone, not only because of the constraints of space, but also as a consequence of a rambling 'free-spirited' nature. However, that's not to say boaters are inherently sad and lonely. Many boaters live aboard with a partner and occasionally whole families live aboard too. Neither are most boaters single. In fact, the novelty of living aboard is often an attractive positive in the dating stakes, and given that most boat folk are 'interesting' people, there is usually no shortage of dating opportunity. On the flip side, it can be difficult to reconcile a constant-cruising or itinerant boating lifestyle with a house-living, land-loving partner, and usually something has to give.

Laundrette list

The Aylesbury Canal Society publishes a list of laundrettes conveniently located near canals and rivers. Find out more at aylesburycanal.org.uk.

Clean clothes

Due to the constraints of space, power and water, most boats do not have a washing machine or tumble dryer on board. Unless you know a friendly neighbourhood washing machine owner you will need to take your dirty washing to a laundrette. Prices vary a little but probably outweigh the cost and inconvenience of running a washing machine on board. 'I always leave my laundry as a service wash,' says Darren from *Dunster*. 'I have much better things to do than spend two hours watching my underwear go round. I'd rather pay an extra couple of pounds and collect it later, washed, dried and folded.'

Some mooring providers, usually the more expensive and luxurious ones, have self-service laundry facilities on site, but these are rare. Usually these are coin-operated laundrette-style machines, but sometimes they are simply standard household models and cost a couple of quid in cash paid to the marina owner. In a bid to solve the problem of not having access to a tumble dryer some boats even have collapsible clothes lines installed near the tiller on their boat.

Transport

Cruising is great so long as you are not reliant upon a car for the duration. Otherwise it can be quite a headache to ensure that both car and boat are in the same place. Once your day of boating fun is over you will need to factor in some way of collecting your car from where you left it, which can mean getting a lift, using a bicycle or using public transport. Either way, collecting a car will cost you time, money, favours or energy and possibly a combination of each. Once again, preparation is key. Finding out about local bus and rail services is probably the easiest solution, providing the services are reliable. Weekends and evenings can often make a mockery of the timetables, especially in rural areas. Cycling back to your car might be an option if you only moved your boat a short distance, and those fit enough to undertake longer journeys might not need to use a car in the first place.

Tony's Towpath Tales

About three years ago I gave my car away to a fellow boater who had more need for it, and I haven't missed it one bit. As a writer I work from my office aboard my boat and do not need a car for commuting. I'm lucky that my mooring is within walking distance of a local train station, and there are shops and a couple of small supermarkets less than a mile away. When I do need a car for long journeys or multi-stop trips I will generally hire one. The combined cost of public transport and occasional car hire is far less than the cost of owning a car, even when that car was parked up and unused for most of the year.

On the whole, I found driving and car ownership to be a stressful and costly headache and not at all suited to my boating lifestyle and philosophy. Tax, insurance, repairs and fuel were eye-wateringly expensive. Road rage and city driving send stress levels through the roof, and so help you if you inadvertently fall foul of one of the many motoring hazards. Parking fines, congestion charges and speed cameras are all expensive and stressful issues to consider, and even the most conscientious and law-abiding drivers can get caught out. But the worst danger is the risk of death and injury if you have an accident. The risks are just too high, and to my mind the odds are not favourable. Even if you are not hurt, the stress and financial implications of an accident make car ownership too unpleasant a prospect for my liking.

My favoured mode of transport these days is a bicycle. For less than £50 I have a reliable and extremely cheap transport option that is suitable for the vast majority of my needs. It keeps me fit and is infinitely better for the environment too. I can fix most things myself, and should the worst happen and I need to buy a new one, they are widely and cheaply available. I'm with HG Wells when he said, 'When I see an adult on a bicycle I do not despair for the future of the human race.'

Boating problem solver

Run out of gas
This will never happen if you always keep a spare bottle handy. There is no excuse for running out, and so, should it happen, you should consider the inconvenience a lesson. A typical 13kg gas canister will usually last at least a month, so there is plenty of time to replace the empty to have as a spare before the one you just attached runs out.

Run out of water
A full water tank lasts so long that it is easy to forget when it is due to run empty. The situation is worse for those boaters who have tanks without any means to inspect the contents. Keeping a large bottle or other container of water on board will help when you run out of water and need a cup of tea, but running out mid shower while lathered in soap is a monumental pain in the backside. It doesn't happen often, but when it does it makes you wish you had checked your water level before you cracked open the Matey.

Toilet tank full
Cassette toilet users will have a spare cassette at the ready and would be foolish to find themselves in the position of having two full cassettes. Pump-out owners can usually be inventive by making use of pubs or public conveniences, or perhaps being moored next to one of the occasional conveniences provided by British Waterways. Alternatively, keeping a small cassette toilet stashed away for such emergencies will negate the need to disappear into the woods with a shovel.

Water pump broken
These should be considered perishable, so be prepared and have a spare pump ready to fit. It is an easy enough job for even the most reluctant DIYer. In the meantime you will need to rely on bottled water and the kettle for your daily ablutions. If a bed bath, flannel wash or festival shower isn't cutting it, then you will need to find an alternative option. Perhaps you are a member of a local health club or maybe there is a public swimming baths nearby? (If so, showering before you swim is important hygiene etiquette.) Your other option is a solar shower, but things must be bad if it comes to this!

Batteries flat

Of course, your starter battery is protected from being flattened by your battery management system or split-relay device, so surely you can just run your engine and recharge? (Unless it is essential, you should not run your engine while moored between 8pm and 8am, so if you arrive home to no power you might as well just go to bed with a candle and a book.) If somehow your starter battery is flat too, you might need to get a jump-start from a friendly fellow boater. Make sure you have a long set of jump leads for this eventuality. If you are super-prepared you will have purchased your portable jump-starter pre-charged, although don't expect it to keep enough charge to start your engine for more than a few days. Older engines may need more power than these devices can kick out, particularly in wintertime, so beware. Alternatively, you might need to get yourself to a boatyard, where they can plug you into the mains and sort the problem out at the same time. Again, a friendly nearby boater might tow you there in exchange for cake or beer.

Run out of milk/bread/beer/similar

Cruising unknown territories is part of the fun of boating, but it is easy to get caught short with provisions. Preparedness, or the availability of a pushbike and the resolution to use it, should mean that this is usually a rare or temporary problem. Some local shops are listed in some waterways guides, but an Internet connection or smartphone will give access to Google maps for more definitive information – either that or ask a local boater. Some taxi services will pick up supplies and deliver them to you, but most will charge a 'lazy customer' premium for this. Wintertime makes access to some waterways impossible by road, so keeping an eye on the changing weather and choosing a sensible mooring is important. It is still easy to get caught out, though, particularly if your regular mooring spot is quite remote. In that case, either a good four-wheel-drive vehicle or the ability to 'man-up' and deal with it is essential.

Bibliography and Resources

BOOKS

The Adlard Coles Book of Diesel Engines, **by Tim Bartlett** (Adlard Coles Nautical)
Explains in clear, jargon-free English how a diesel engine works, and how to look after it, and takes into account developments in engine technology.

Canals of Britain, **by Stuart Fisher** (Adlard Coles Nautical)
An inspiring, practical guide, which is popular with all canal enthusiasts and boaters wanting to get the most out of Britain's canals.

De-Junk Your Life, **by Helen Foster**
Not specifically aimed at boaters, but the philosophy is well suited to liveaboard life.

The Inland Waterways Logbook, **by Emrhy Barrell** (Adlard Coles Nautical)
This handy, paperback logbook is designed specifically for inland waterways boaters, and contains many useful pages of data.

The Inland Waterways Manual, **by Emrhy Barrell** (Adlard Coles Nautical)
This book will tell the reader all they need to know about how to get afloat – which boat to choose, whether to hire or buy, how much it will cost, and where they can go.

London's Waterways, **by Derek Pratt** (Adlard Coles Nautical)
With its stylish design, beautiful photography and quirky captions, this gorgeous coffee table book is the perfect gift for inland waterways enthusiasts, as well as tourists and Londoners.

Narrowboats, Care and Maintenance, **by Nick Billingham**
A useful breakdown of boat maintenance, and although written in 1995, not much changes on the cut.

Sell Up and Cruise the Inland Waterways, **by Bill Cooper, Laurel Cooper** (Adlard Coles Nautical)
With anecdotes from their own experiences to illustrate their points, as well as maps, sketches and photographs, the Coopers can help anyone dreaming of selling up and cruising the inland waterways to make that dream become a reality.

Voyaging on a small income, **by Annie Hill**
About yachting, but contains some fabulous advice and was the inspiration for this book.

MAGAZINES

Boaters' Handbook
A brilliant concise guide to boat handling and safety. Available as a free booklet from British Waterways and free download available at: http://www.waterscape.com/media/documents/1784.pdf

Buying a Boat, How to Get Started
A good place to start with the basics – practical advice and resources and available free from British Waterways.

Canal Boat
A magazine championing our wonderful waterways and boating for well over a decade, providing news, views, boat tests, practical advice, cruising ideas, updates on canal restorations and keeping everyone in touch with everything that's happening on the UK's canals and rivers.

Canals, Rivers and Boats
A magazine covering many waterways orientated activities, including boating.

Towpath Talk
A popular free monthly newspaper about the UK waterways featuring the latest news, trader ads, waterways stoppages and events.

Waterways World
The biggest-selling and longest-established inland waterways magazine.

CLUBS, SOCIETIES AND OTHER ORGANISATIONS

The Inland Waterways Association
The IWA is a registered charity, founded in 1946, which advocates the conservation, use, maintenance, restoration and development of the inland waterways for public benefit.

The National Association of Boat Owners
NABO is dedicated to promoting the interests of private boaters on Britain's canals, rivers and lakes, so that their voice can be heard when decisions are being made which might affect their boating.

Residential boat owners association
Established in 1963 the Residential Boat Owners' Association is the only national organisation which exclusively represents and promotes the interests of people living on boats in the British Isles. Representing all those who have chosen to make a boat their home – whether that boat is static or cruises; is based inland or on the coast; has a permanent or temporary mooring (whether residential or not) or continuously cruises – all are residential boaters.

ONLINE RESOURCES

The Considerate Boater – www.considerateboater.com
Aiming to promote considerate boating and good boating etiquette on the inland waterways.

Canal Cuttings – www.canalcuttings.co.uk
A free online boating magazine. Over 750 pages of information and features about canals, navigable rivers and their usage including classified and waterside property ads.

Granny Buttons – www.grannybuttons.com
An entertaining and illuminating blog by boater and journalist Andrew Denny with the strapline 'My own private thoughts and ignorance about the canals and waterways. (And no-one else's, except as quoted.)'

Low Impact Life On Board – www.liloontheweb.org.uk
The LILO website is where you'll find information about the eco-boating community in Britain.

LARGE BOAT BROKERAGES

Apollo Duck – www.apolloduck.co.uk
Online Brokerage – Large site with thousands of boats and related items for sale.

Boats and Outboards – www.boatsandoutboards.co.uk
Online brokerage — Find thousands of boats for sale and other boating related ads.

Whilton Marina
Whilton Marina is located at Whilton Locks near Daventry on the Grand Union Canal. The company has been buying, selling and caring for narrow boats since 1971 and have a large selection of narrow boats for sale at the marina for viewing.
Address: Whilton Locks near Daventry, Northamptonshire NN11 2NH
Tel: 01327 842577
Email: sales@whiltonmarina.co.uk
Web: www.whiltonmarina.co.uk

OTHER

NHS Direct
For health advice and reassurance 24 hours a day, 365 days a year.
Tel: 0845 46 47
Web: www.nhsdirect.nhs.uk

INDEX